P9-CLP-949

RELIGION AND POLITICS IN AMERICA

Religion and Politics in America

Murray S. Stedman, Jr.

A Harbinger Book
HARCOURT, BRACE & WORLD
NEW YORK • BURLINGAME

To EMILY *and* NANCY

Library of Congress Catalog Card Number: 64-19366

Printed in the United States of America

Preface

Periodically, issues involving the role of the churches and that of the state assume unusual significance in public discussion and legislative debate. Recent decisions of the Supreme Court and proposals before Congress for various kinds of federal assistance to education—to say nothing of the religious undertones of Presidential and other campaigns—have once again catapulted the phrase "religion and politics" into general usage.

The actual relationships between religious forces and those of government have long interested historians and social scientists. Ordinarily, the objective of scholarly investigators has been to describe these relationships in order to understand more precisely how religion affects politics.

At a different level of inquiry, there has persisted a concern with the question of what ought to be the role of the churches in the total political process. What is involved here is an investigation into political theory. The inquirers in this instance are seeking out an ideal of behavior against which they can weigh and measure the actual behavior of the churches.

The purpose of this book is to advance an understanding of the relationships between religion and politics on both the empirical and the theoretical level. In pursuing this objective materials have been cited from all periods of American history, but the bulk of the illustrations date from the end of the Second World War.

It is my conviction that the churches have played and are playing an important part in the continuing development of democratic theory and practice in America. In that sense this is a book about democracy.

I wish to express my gratitude to several friends who read the original manuscript and offered suggestions which clearly improved the final text. They are Samuel Hendel of The City College of New York, Eve McFall of the National Council of Churches, C. Ellis Nelson of Union Theological Seminary in New York, John P. Roche of Brandeis University, and James F. Tierney of the Ford Foundation. My wife, Susan W. Stedman, has been helpful, in ways too numerous to detail, throughout the completion of this undertaking.

Finally, I should like to note that Chapter Four, "Accommodation and Conflict in Church-State Relations," first appeared in slightly different form as an article under the title of "Church, State, People: The Eternal Triangle." It is here reprinted by special permission from the *Western Political Quarterly*, September 1963.

MURRAY S. STEDMAN, JR.

February 19, 1964

Contents

CHAPTER ONE

The Pattern of Religion and Politics

Public reaction to the Supreme Court's decision in 1962 in the Regents' Prayer case,[1] which outlawed the recitation of a nondenominational prayer in the public schools of New York State, was sharp, bitter, and sarcastic. To some clergymen, this must have seemed somewhat hypocritical, for up to that point this same public had been silent in its opinion on the efficacy of prayer in general and in the schools in particular. The very emotional reaction engendered by the Court's decision persisted through the hot summer months but was dissipated with the passage of time.

A year later the Supreme Court came to grips with two related and much more potentially explosive issues. At stake were a Pennsylvania statute requiring the reading of ten verses from the Bible at the opening of each public school on each school day and a rule of the Baltimore school commissioners, based on Maryland law, that provided for both daily reading from the Bible and recitation of the Lord's Prayer. On June 17, 1963, the Supreme Court, with one justice dissenting, declared that the practices under attack constituted violations of the establishment clause of the First Amendment, as applied to the states through the Fourteenth Amendment.[2]

As expected, the reaction was loud and pained. Yet it was not sustained, and the question arose as to what had happened since the decision in the Regents' Prayer case to mollify public opinion. Several factors appeared to be responsible. Some justices of the Supreme Court, disturbed by the charges of antireligious prejudice leveled at them following the New York State case, had gone to great lengths in their speeches to indicate that the decision had been widely misunderstood. Also of great importance was the acceptance of the Regents' Prayer decision and its implications by various responsible religious bodies. At first hostile, the National Association of Evangelicals came to accept the church-state philosophy upon which the decision was based. In May of 1963, the General Assembly of the United Presbyterian Church, meeting in Des Moines, passed a resolution that accurately anticipated the Court's decisions a month later. The statement endorsed principles that called for the outlawing of Bible reading and the recitation of the Lord's Prayer as religious exercises in the public schools. The Presbyterian proclamation stirred up a storm of criticism, as no doubt had been expected, but it also served as a lightning rod to divert some of the highly charged emotion from the Court itself to a particular church body. A few weeks after the Presbyterian action the National Council of Churches made a somewhat ambiguous statement that, on balance, was consonant with the principles of the Supreme Court's forthcoming decisions.

In this fashion, over the period of a year, the groundwork was laid for a shift in public opinion. The public had been warned of what the Court was likely to do. When it did what had been expected, there was a great deal of criticism at first, but only a few expressed complete dismay.

The issue of how much and what kind of religion to have in the public schools is and will continue to be a problem. The relationship between religion and politics is complex, and even recent Supreme Court decisions have not served to clarify fully the First Amendment. The relationship, too, is in motion, and is changing, and it is often difficult to sight the buoys amidst the waves. This relationship between religion and politics can be best understood as a process. "Process" implies movement, and does not exclude an element of rationality or of direction; in this context, it also implies a situation of reciprocity, and brings to mind action and counteraction and reaction.

The relationship between church and state, both as defined by the Constitution and as actually practiced, has always been of great importance in American society.[3] Religion and politics do constitute a good part of human experience, and the two concepts are so interrelated that it is often difficult to separate them. Yet the relationship can be understood more clearly if each term is defined separately. Each term has its particular difficulties, of course. "Politics" as used here includes the whole political process—from the individual who makes up his mind in a political situation to such stable institutions as courts and legislatures. "Religion," in its broadest meaning, includes ideas people hold about the nature and meaning of the universe and its parts. So broad a definition is not, however, especially useful. "Religion" is understood here to mean systems of belief about man and his relationship with God held by people and institutionalized through continuing associations, or churches. The focus is, then, on people, as organized into churches, and the relationships between such organizations and the political process.

The relationship between religion and politics is obviously relevant and current and important, as it has been in preceding generations. There is, indeed, a good deal of reason to believe that the tensions generated by actual or potential religious-political disagreement are greater in our day than they have been for some time, especially on the question of aid to schools. It is possible, of course, that an accommodation will be reached on this issue, and that passions will cool. The question remains, however, whether the over-all relationship between religion and politics, until now an important one, will continue to be so. In assessing this problem, it is only necessary to concentrate on religion, for politics will continue as long as *Homo sapiens* does.

Most ordinary citizens, if asked their opinions, would undoubtedly predict without hesitation that religion will continue to be important as an element on the American social and political scene. The only reason they might hesitate at all, in venturing an answer, would be because they know some of the country's contemporary religious experts have serious reservations about the future of religion.

Some of them have declared that religion as practiced in America is obsolete. One of the speakers before the fourth World Conference on Faith and Order, which met in Montreal in July 1963 was the Rev. Dr. Robert E. Cushman, Dean of the Duke University Divinity School. This distinguished churchman, as reported by the Associated Press, told his audience that "worship has become largely meaningless."[4] The dispatch continued: "Worship is becoming a cloistered exercise of the pious, conducted by punctilious professionals." There was more in this vein, but these words are representative. Lest it be thought that Dean Cushman is unique in his castigation of modern Christian practice in the United States, let it be observed that the so-called angry young men of the cloth—such prolific writers as Gibson Winter, Peter Berger, and Martin Marty—also spend much of their public lives in warning laymen of the superficiality of the churches in this country.[5]

The constitutional right of churchmen to criticize the churches is, of course, guaranteed under the First Amendment of the Constitution, and, in any event, there is a long and honorable Biblical genealogy to this custom. Yet it must strike one as unusual, to say the least, when a leading physician criticizes in the newspapers the American Medical Association, or when a member of the airline pilots guild suggests that his colleagues do not know how to handle planes. Perhaps what limits the effectiveness of Dean Cushman and the other critics of modern religion is that, ordinarily, only the other professionals take them literally. For the evidence is that organized religion (even if not of the precise quality that the critics would like) is not dying, and will continue vigorously to affect the political process in the United States for many years to come.

CHURCH MEMBERSHIP: DENOMINATIONAL DISTRIBUTION

Religious affiliation is a central, not a marginal, characteristic of modern American life. According to the *Yearbook of American Churches* for 1963 (which reported totals through the calendar year 1961), there are in the United States some 116 million church members.[6] When classified by major groups, they are divided in this way: Protestants, 64.4 million; Roman Catholics, 42.8 million; Jews, 5.3 million; Eastern Orthodox, 2.8 million; Old Catholics, Polish National Catholics, and Armenians, 572,000.

The degree of cohesiveness in a particular group is of potential significance in politics; in this respect Roman Catholicism is in the best position. Protestantism and Judaism are both divided, the former spectacularly so. The *Yearbook* reports the existence of approximately 250 Protestant religious groups. Judaism is split along Orthodox, Conservative, and Reformed lines.

Yet both Protestantism and Judaism are less fragmented than over-all statistics might imply. Jews are widely brought together under the Synagogue Council, and Protestants through the National Council of the Churches of Christ in the U.S.A. The NCC includes in its membership some thirty-one communions, of which seven are Eastern Orthodox Churches, for a combined constituency of 40.3 million. The two largest Protestant groups not in the NCC are the Southern Baptist Convention, with approximately 10 million members, and the Lutheran Church-Missouri Synod, with 2.4 million. Other sizable non–Roman Catholic bodies—which are outside the Protestant conciliar movement—are the Mormons, Jehovah's Witnesses, and the various Pentecostal and Holiness sects.

The distribution of the adherents to a particular faith is also of potential significance. Here Roman Catholicism is at a disadvantage, for despite its very large membership, the group is distributed unevenly across the country. Catholics constitute an absolute majority of the population only in Rhode Island. The characteristics of distribution also, of course, affect other religious groups. Presbyterianism is largely divided into Northern and Southern branches, in an unhealed schism growing out of the Civil War. The Southern Baptists are, as the title implies, mostly a regional denomination. Mormonism is at its strongest in Utah and the other Mountain states. There are also definite class and economic differences that separate many of the non-Catholic religious bodies. For these reasons it is misleading to assess Protestant strength or potential strength purely on the basis of numbers. The numerical unity so implied would in most cases prove to be illusory when measured against the harsh realities of election or referenda returns. (Some Protestants, for instance, believe with Jonathan Edwards that rum in moderation is a blessing of God; others are convinced that alcohol is an invention of Satan. It is difficult to reconcile these views on the ground that those who hold them are all Protestants! In other words, it is much easier to describe and define the Protestant churches of America individually than to define Protestantism generally.)

The principal faiths—Protestantism, Catholicism, and Judaism—each evidence certain signs of weakness because of geography or lack of inherent unity. When measured against the total population, no single church even remotely approaches having on its membership rolls a majority of the nation's people. Yet, taken as a whole, the religious movement of the last two decades has exhibited a growth and a vitality that are the more remarkable because they were so unexpected. The boom in membership and in amount of funds since 1945 has been unique in American history. In 1850, church members constituted 16 per cent of the population; at the end of 1961, 63.4 per cent. During 1960, some 47 Protestant and Orthodox churches reported contributions of more than two and a half billion dollars.

The health of the churches, as measured in the statistics of membership and of funds, never appeared more vigorous than at the start of the 1960's. There were, to be sure, critics who dismissed the "religious revival" as primarily mere "religiosity," a highly developed form of keeping up with the

Joneses. Yet thoughtful churchmen never expected the religious boom to go on forever. As students of ecclesiastical history, they felt certain that in a free society there must be some limits to growth in church membership and in church funds. They were therefore neither surprised nor depressed when the *Yearbook* for 1963 hinted that the postwar religious revival had reached its high-water mark and was beginning to recede. According to the *Yearbook*, the percentage of American people claiming church membership dropped for the first time in one hundred years. The drop was minuscule—only 0.2 percentage points—but it did indicate that the increase in church membership was lagging behind population growth.[7] There was also reported a modest decline in the value of new church construction.[8]

A leveling off in church growth, even if continued for some years, would not necessarily mean a decline in church influence on matters of public policy. Under any reasonable projection of trends, a large majority of American men, women, and children will be church-related during the foreseeable future. But church membership alone, while one measure of influence, is not the most important criterion. Other factors, depending on the particular circumstances, would be the commitment of church members to church-endorsed political goals, the political skill and talent of church leaders, and the ability of churchmen of different backgrounds and denominations to achieve operational unity. In addition to such internal factors, certain external conditions in the society as a whole would affect the political role of church groups (as they would influence that of other groups): whether we were at war or not, what the condition of the economy was, how content we were with the status quo. And, of course, the freedom of action of any one group is obviously limited and usually checked by the freedom of action of other associations.

The probability, then, is that the churches will neither grow until they come to dominate the affairs of the Republic, nor dwindle in membership and become ineffectual. They will remain what they have been, which is to say, vigorous, voluntary, self-financing associations. They will operate, for the most part, under the traditional "rules of the game" that have defined the conditions of American political activity.

TRENDS IN RELIGIOUS AFFILIATION

The religious community is, of course, divided into many different denominations, sects, and movements, which hold varying and often contrasting ideas as to political action. Quantitative, or membership, changes inside the religious community may therefore have qualitative effects. A vast changing of denominational preference from old-line Protestant denominations to the Jehovah's Witnesses sect, for example, would probably result in a serious shift of opinion on the question of America's participation in the United Nations. Similarly, a large-scale shift inside the Jewish community from Reformed to Orthodox preference would have important repercussions regarding the applicability of Sunday closing laws.

In fact, changes in religious affiliation take place gradually and over extended periods of time. Nonetheless, changes do take place, and they may be expected to have some effect on attitudes toward politics. We can project with some accuracy future political attitudes: when we know the rates of growth of individual denominations and their historic attitudes for or against social action, we can correlate the two factors.

Over the last half century the single most impressive feature on the American religious scene has been the growth of Roman Catholicism. Its growth has been especially marked if one considers that much of the Protestant growth in the last two decades has represented a shift from mere Protestant preference to active membership in Protestant churches. While Protestantism was winning back erring sheep, Catholicism (through immigration and a higher birth rate) was adding to its own flock.

The attitudes of American Catholicism toward social action have been ambivalent. Yet there is no doubt that social encyclicals of the Popes since the last part of the nineteenth century have encouraged, in America as elsewhere, a positive concern for the achievement of social justice through governmental means. Pope John XXIII, especially, encouraged this tendency. It is reasonable to expect that American Catholicism will grow in numbers and in prestige and that it will increasingly make its views felt on a wide variety of social and political issues.

In contrast, the main-line Protestant denominations—such as the Episcopalians, the Methodists, and the two principal Presbyterian bodies—are growing very slowly. They are not, in fact, keeping pace with the birth rate. These denominations—along with several other old-line groups—are at the very core of the modern cooperative movement. They founded the National Council of Churches and they are its principal support. The National Council, which engages in many activities as the agent of its members, is the main social action agency of cooperative American Protestantism.

Several denominations that stand outside the National Council, notably the Southern Baptists, are growing at a much faster rate than the old-line denominations inside the National Council. The significance of this observation, of course, lies in the traditional distrust on the part of Southern Baptists of much of the social action which has been so distinctive of the cooperative movement.

Finally, the largest increases in membership of all religious groups in the United States have for some years been registered by Holiness and Pentecostal sects, which are outside the mainstream of American Protestantism. In general, these groups view social action, especially in the political sector, as a waste of time. What can be hazarded as a prediction—if present trends and conditions continue—is that those Protestant churches that have historically opposed social action will become even more prominent, while the social action–oriented denominations become less influential; the latter will probably face a period of relative decline in numbers. If sustained, these trends could mean increased Protestant political support for the status quo and thus a diminution in the overall effectiveness of the Protestant churches as social critics.

A Note on "Social Action" and the "Cooperative Movement"

"Social action" and the "cooperative movement" are very different concepts, even though it seems natural to link them in ordinary discourse. The objective of social action by the churches is to use church influence to alter certain conditions in society. Often this calls for changes in public policy through writing new laws or changing old ones. When church forces engage in drives to improve the climate of international relations or to alter the American educational system or to press for the enactment of prohibition laws, they are involved in social action. Confusion arises not so much over the nature of this kind of church activity as over the objectives that are sought. Where actions are considered to be matters of individual morality—as with the consumption of alcohol or public dancing or the use of lipstick—opponents of the campaign in question will be likely to label it "pietistic," meaning they disapprove. Where governmental action intended to broaden or secure the rights of certain groups is required—for example, voter registration laws to make it easier for Negroes to vote—opponents are likely to charge that the church forces are "outside" the concerns of religion. They say that the clergymen and the churches "should stick to preaching religion."

In our time, the churches that constitute the cooperative, or "conciliar," movement, that is, who are members of the National Council of Churches, have through their governing assemblies been closely associated with social action which requires governmental intervention. As a general rule, those churches which have remained outside the movement have maintained that the reform of individual church members will lead to eventual social reform. Even so, these same churches may insist that government pass and enforce certain types of laws, notably those that restrict the conduct of an individual. And, of course, not all church members within the movement are firmly committed to vigorous social action, nor are those outside the movement firmly opposed to such action.

THE CONSTITUTIONAL AND POLITICAL FRAMEWORK

A relative decline in the strength of the old-line Protestant bodies in itself would not result in any sudden or revolutionary transformation in the role of the churches in American politics. A really drastic shift could come about only through altering the United States Constitution or through changes of the most profound sort inside the churches.

With the sole exception of the Civil War, the American constitutional system has managed to contain political activity within peaceful limits. It has done so by establishing and enforcing certain ground rules that govern the behavior of contestants for power. The rules apply to the churches, as to other social institutions, and they limit what the churches may do in the area of politics and, equally important, what the government may do in the area of religion.

The churches enjoy the same privileges of freedom of association as do other groups. They are voluntary, tax-exempt, and self-governing. But the churches have an additional advantage that is accorded to them just because they are the institutional embodiment of religion. Under the First Amendment (now applied to the states through the Fourteenth Amendment), religion enjoys a large degree of constitutional immunity from government. The First Amendment declares in part: "Congress shall make no law respecting an establishment of religion, or prohibiting the free exercise thereof . . ." In practice this has meant that government at all levels has ordinarily shown a benevolent neutrality toward religious institutions.

The phrase usually used to describe this constitutional arrangement is "separation of church and state," a phrase that is far less clear than it may seem to be at first glance. The arrangement is an American innovation, not the American adaptation of an old European Protestant doctrine.

The Government's Benevolent Neutrality

American culture emphasizes the symbolic significance of religion both as an important element in American culture and as an adjunct of patriotism, and the American people have, for the most part, expected that government would be helpful to religion in a number of ways not involving sectarianism and not implying direct subsidization of the churches. There is nothing in the least mysterious about this attitude, for the American people know that religion helped form American culture and they believe it performs an essential role in binding together American society. They also believe, as they have been taught since childhood to believe, that religion provides purposeful significance to national history. (It is quite likely that much of the outcry against the Supreme Court decisions on Bible reading and prayer in the public schools stemmed from the belief of the "average" man that the Supreme Court did not understand the historic functions of religion in American life!)

The result of this web of constitutional arrangements has been, until now at least, more than satisfactory for the churches. The situation is equally advantageous from the government's point of view. It is therefore difficult to see what if anything would be gained, either by the government or by the churches, through drastic constitutional surgery. It is easy—as Robert MacIver pointed out long ago—to imagine conditions under which democratic government could not possibly continue, conditions which might tend to result in its overthrow and replacement by some other form of government.[9] No doubt, the government itself would take a dim view of its overthrow. As for the churches, the history of this century has shown how much they would stand to lose. For any self-respecting totalitarian government either crushes the churches or makes them insofar as feasible the lackeys of the regime. The churches, at the very least, would find their freedom of action shackled.

Religious Dissatisfaction and Political Extremists

Barring some cataclysm that would bring existing society—its governmental and social institutions—to the brink of ruin, it is likely that the present constitutional arrangements between government and the leading social institutions will be in general maintained. It remains possible, however, that dissatisfaction within the churches could reach such a pitch that there would be demands to alter the existing constitutional relationship.[10]

Religious dissatisfaction often serves largely to disguise objectives sought by social and political malcontents. As Alan Westin and other commentators have noted, it is more than a concidence that the most intemperate critics of the social positions of the National Council of Churches have been flag-waving, fundamentalist, right-wing politicians.[11] Extreme right-wing politics and extreme right-wing religion find much in common, and often the latter merely serves as a smoke screen to hide the former from exposure. Both are often associated with anti-Negro and anti-Jewish manifestations as well as with highly restricted views of the role of government in the economy.

Racism exists in all parts of the Republic, but it is much more virulent in the South than in the North, in rural than in urban areas, among white Protestants than among white Catholics. Protestant racism—as a self-conscious force—is obviously of considerable magnitude in many Southern states, and is the predominant ideological factor in Mississippi and in Alabama. What is less obvious is that unself-conscious white Protestant racism was widespread, taken for granted, and largely unchallenged in many sections of the Union until the rise of the Negro civil-rights movement in the late 1950's.

The irony of the situation, from the religious point of view, lay in the fact that it was Negro Protestants who exposed widespread prejudice in the beliefs and habits of white Protestants. It was Negro Protestants who, as it were, compelled their "moderate" (that is, apathetic) white coreligionists to put up or shut up. It was Negro Protestants who pointed out that the high-sounding principles of racial equality so ringingly endorsed by white Protestant denominations were largely ignored in ordinary life by their white communicants. It was the Negro Protestants who suggested that contemporary white Protestantism, in the area of racial problems at least, was an anachronism.

Stung by these charges, non-Southern white Protestant leaders—as represented on the General Board of the National Council of Churches—took dramatic, if eleventh-hour action, in June 1963. At that time, the Board voted to associate itself with negotiations, lobbying, and street demonstrations on behalf of civil rights for Negroes, and pledged the active support of Board members as individuals. In addition, the Board urged its member communions to take parallel action.

In capsule form, the major stages in the great social dialectic were these: the white Protestants of the South as religionists did little or nothing to implement the 1954 school-case decisions of the Supreme Court; Negro Protestants (acting in most cases outside their denominations and through educational or civic organizations) took the initiative first by challenging segregation patterns in the South and then by opposing discrimination in other parts of the country; the great, old-line, white-dominated Protestant denominations voted (through their national assemblies) to join actively with the Negro organizations in a common struggle for Negro civil rights.

The whole development illustrates how the extremes (Southern whites, opposed to change, and Negroes, agitating for change) can goad the middle-of-the-roaders (non-Southern white Protestant leaders) into action. Should the middle-of-the-road effort fail because it is too late, or too little, or simply because it is not heeded by the great masses of white Protestants, the possibilities increase that powerful religious forces may demand a restatement of the religion-politics relationship. Such a restatement could conceivably take several forms, one of which, for instance, might be the insistence by a religious body that certain communal rights be guaranteed by the state. A demand of this sort might arise if a large religious group felt that the ordinary methods of political action would not result in the achievement of its objectives. The solution of isolation with certain guarantees might appear welcome. While this is an unlikely example, it is not necessarily hyperbolic. The Black Muslims, in demanding a separate state, show the extremes to which an ethnic-religious group can go.

Calamitous economic and political conditions or the rise of large-scale religious extremist groups could, in short, result in agitation effective enough to change the traditional American model of the relationship between politics and religion. Either set of circumstances is, of course, quite logically possible, and would mean the end of the constitutional and political framework as it has prevailed up to now. Yet the probabilities obviously favor the continuation of the existing framework.

THE JUDGMENTAL ROLE OF THE CHURCHES

This framework sets, in a general way, limits to what the churches can and cannot do in the political arena. On the positive side, the churches can govern themselves, finance themselves, and proselytize to their hearts' content. They may lobby (even if they refrain from using the exact word in order to observe the letter but violate the spirit of the law); they may try to influence public opinion; they may intervene (in Sunday closing referenda, for example) in the electoral process. However, the churches are limited by the realities of the political world in certain important respects. Practically, they cannot sponsor and control political parties (as happens in some European countries), and no one church, therefore, can hope to control the government. In effect, this limitation restricts the political role of religious leaders. An individual minister or rabbi may be elected to a school board, or even to Congress, but he serves as an individual, not as the agent of a church-sponsored political party.

Under the American arrangement, it is also fairly difficult for a church to push particular bills pending before a legislature, and it is often dangerous to do so. Opposition to the bill will almost surely turn into opposition to the religious groups that support the bill. A church is on "safest" ground when, from its own point of view, it speaks to the "morality" of certain legislation. It is on very slippery ground when it comments on the general "desirability" of legislation.

These specifics add up to the general contention that the churches cannot control politics, even potentially. They are not organized into political parties and they cannot be organized into parties. Their influence on politics must ordinarily, therefore, be indirect. It is often maintained that these restrictions on church power in politics stem primarily from the diversity of religious groups in the United States. It is held that a church is kept in place not because it lacks confidence in its ability to run society but because other churches will not permit it to do so. This contention, founded on a "realistic" approach to human nature which a John Adams would have found congenial, fails to do justice to our constitutional law and history. The constitutional arrangements in effect in Utah, for example, do not permit the Mormon Church to confuse its present position with that of the Puritan establishment in the Massachusetts Bay Colony in the seventeenth century.

The same constitutional limitations that affect churches as corporate bodies also serve to inhibit the political role of religious leaders. Clearly, any prominent religious figure has the right to stand for public office, or to comment on what laws he would like to see Congress or a state legislature consider and pass. In most instances, such behavior would certainly be considered distasteful by large elements of the general public.[12] Such a feeling involves a good deal more than mere "anticlericalism," for it is difficult to find much avowed anticlericalism in the American public. (Anticlericalism thrives where there is an established church, not under conditions of religious pluralism.) In part the distaste would and does arise from a belief that a clergyman who offers himself as a political leader is overstepping the boundaries of the domains of church and state. However theologically unsound, the general understanding is that political leadership should be left to the politicans, and that religious leaders should attend to religion. There is, in addition, an element of fair play involved in the general public's assessment of clergymen as political leaders.

It is widely believed, for instance, that Representative Adam Clayton Powell cannot at the same time fulfill the duties assigned to the Reverend Adam Clayton Powell. To many Americans, there is more than a touch of the medieval in the Harlem clergyman's blending of church and state in his person.

As a practical matter, then, neither present public opinion nor past public opinion as embedded in institutional patterns will permit the churches or their chiefs to assume significant leadership in political affairs. (The Prohibition movement is a special case and does not violate this tenet.)

In addition to the judgmental role, what roles do the public and the churches themselves consider appropriate for church bodies and church officials?

It is, and always has been, deemed proper and appropriate for the churches to engage in a wide variety of educational activities, including education that has political overtones. Usually, of course, any overt political objective has been hidden in nonpolitical terminology. The Methodist-sponsored Church Center for the United Nations, for example, is dedicated to the maintenance of peace, not primarily to the United Nations, which is considered a means to that end. Roman Catholic objections to the dissemination of birth control devices to women on relief are based on considerations of "natural law" or on a desire to maintain chastity, not on a desire to impose by political pressure the will of one group on others.

Churches expect to affect behavior and attitudes through religious education. It is anticipated that deductions from general principles will be applicable to social, economic, or political situations. In general, neither the government nor the public will interfere with or object to the educational program of a religious group. They will object only when efforts are made to transform sectarian beliefs of the group into public law.

The churches may educate but they may not actively participate—these are the general political limitations placed upon them. There is one other function that the churches may and sometimes do perform—a function for which in principle they are better prepared than other groups in society—which is to examine a political situation or proposal dispassionately and then to pass judgment on it. This function is by definition more judicial than executive or legislative and is somewhat alien to the traditions of the churches, especially the Protestant churches, of America. In a culture where even the churches are characterized by hypertense activism, it is difficult to find churchmen, let alone church institutions, competent to perform in any mature sense a judgmental role.

It is unfortunate that this is so, for the churches have at least two advantages over labor, education, and the press when it comes to passing judgment on significant political happenings. The first advantage is a sense of moral awareness, an ability to grasp the moral implications of great issues. Certainly such awareness is not evenly distributed among church officials and religious groups, and cynics may wonder if it exists at all. Yet it would be conceded by most persons that specialists in ethics (which is one way of looking at ministers, priests, and rabbis) have more expertise than nonspecialists.

In addition, religious bodies have a greater sense of history, on the average, than do labor unions, schools and universities, or the organs of mass communications. Not only that—they also have a greater sense of the continuity of human development than do most other institutions. Church leaders are less likely to be affected by day-to-day happenings than are other people. They have a sense of perspective that is essential for sound judgment.

The churches may, of course, arrive after a good deal of thought at judgments which, when viewed retrospectively, appear incorrect or even ridiculous, but so may governments, business establishments, trades unions, football teams, political parties, and newspapers.

So far as significant issues of public policy are concerned, the contention is that the churches and their leaders are and ought to be able to pass judgments that are intrinsically superior to those of other institutions and leaders because the churches have a greater awareness of moral consequences and a more profound grasp of history.

Both theologians and cultural determinists would examine the judgmental role of the churches under different sets of lenses from those used by political theorists. However, it is quite evident that churchmen contribute handsomely to the democratic political process when they pass mature judgment on government and politics on religious grounds. For pragmatic as well as theoretical reasons, it is therefore highly desirable that this aspect of the relationship between religion in America and American politics be continued and be further developed. The prospect is that this will happen.

CHAPTER TWO

Limitations on the Political Activity of Religion

The freedom of the churches to engage in the various forms of political activity is under law virtually unlimited. In practice, the limitations are very real. They stem from the inhibitions that society places upon all social institutions merely because it is in society that they exist at all. The fact that these restrictions are not always apparent or self-evident in no sense negates their reality or effectiveness. Indeed, the invisible demands of society may be more tyrannical than the most brazenly declared abuses of dictators.

If religion is to be relevant to the political situation, it must usually be so under inherited conditions that are only partly of its own making. Religion, which is, though of great importance, only one of many forces operating in society, must arrive at some kind of a modus vivendi with the other basic institutions, especially government. There are certain factors that condition what religious organizations may or may not do in the society as a whole, and there are identifiable factors that condition what religion may do in the political arena. The effectiveness of religious forces in politics will be determined by the degree of harmony or disharmony of these influencing factors.

Religious organizations could if they chose make use of all or most of the same political devices and methods as other interest groups. Such methods run the spectrum from education to participation. It probably does not make much practical difference to the man who has no vote whether a voter-registration drive is carried on under the auspices of a church or of a civic group. To the active, informed voter, however, it may make a good deal of difference. An oil lobby working hard to have birth control legislation enacted would seem as out of character as a church lobby working hard to have petroleum quotas established by law. Voter-registration drives, while not necessarily ethically "neutral," would qualify under the heading of education. Pressure to pass a particular bill, even if exerted in the name of the "public interest," is by definition divisive. Nonpartisan groups, such as the churches, usually wish to pass judgment on the principles of legislation while leaving the details to the legislators. More than merely a public "image" is involved, for the judgmental role is, as we have seen, of great actual and potential value in itself.

Some political functions performed by religious groups are simple, some are complex, and some are in between. But none can be performed effectively unless the churches possess and exercise a very real degree of independence from the other leading institutions of society. Independence is not to be confused with mere opposition; an independent role calls for an intelligent and continuing perspective. If the churches were to consider themselves or to behave as merely an adjunct of the going system, they would not matter much, politically, to very many people.

THE CHURCHES' FREEDOM FROM EXTERNAL CONTROLS

Even if the churches of America feel very strongly that they should affect political and social processes, they would still be unable to do so unless certain conditions were present in society. Externally these conditions include relative freedom from political, economic, and class control, and from society's value-systems.

Political Control

Freedom from political control is relatively easy to deal with, for on this point American beliefs and American customs are in tune. It has almost always been recognized that state control of the churches was, under American conditions, bad for the churches. It took somewhat longer for the conviction to grow that church control of the state was also bad for the churches. In time, this thesis, the rationale of which was superbly spelled out by Roger Williams, became accepted as an essential element of the American creed by the dominant religious groups in our society.[1]

Economic Control

Freedom from economic control has been more difficult for the churches to achieve. Part of the difficulty is attributable to the concept that "he who pays the piper calls the tune," which may mean both that the piper does and ought to call the tune. We are told repeatedly, for example, that it would be immoral for the federal government to supply funds for public schools unless some measure of governmental control were instituted. The argument is that it is unethical and monetarily irresponsible to give money away without first attaching very tight strings, and, oppositely, that a church ought not to criticize people and institutions if it receives money from them.

It is easier to make this argument stick in a homogeneous rural society where the churches, whatever their formal type of government, are congregational in character, than it is in a heterogeneous urban society. The rise of vast national denominations, too, has made it more difficult to discover for exactly what purpose a specific dollar put into the collection plate was ultimately spent. The impersonality of money and the anonymity of bigness conspire to make it difficult for even the largest of individual church contributors to exercise a veto over denominational expenditures. In addition, there is so much money involved from so many sources that an individual donor's contribution to the total cannot be very large.

When a sizable number of laymen pool their financial resources, the threat to the independence of the church bodies increases correspondingly. An example of this type of threatened coercion took place early in the life of the National Council of Churches. When the Council was about to be formed late in 1950, a number of church leaders, worried over ways to finance the Council, asked several laymen of means for financial assistance. A Lay Committee was established for this purpose, but it moved rapidly from financial discussions to social pronouncements. The Committee took the position that it should have a veto power over social statements and resolutions taken by the denominationally elected governing General Board. The Board decided that it, as the representative of the communions, would retain the final say, and the Committee subsequently went out of existence.

In the late 1950's a series of similar attempts was made to force the General Assembly of the United Presbyterian Church to accede to the views of certain prominent industrialists on pain of withholding contributions. Churchmen—both clerical and lay—lost their tempers. *Presbyterian Life* in sternest tones told oil magnate J. Howard Pew to inform his rich friends that the General Assembly was "not for sale."[2] Statisticians at the denomination's headquarters noted, however, that the upward trend in financial contributions to national causes of the denomination had continued without interruption. It was even surmised by Presbyterian publicists that some small contributors might have increased their giving to offset the decreases anticipated on the part of "Mr. Pew's friends."

Class Control

Another conditioning factor, one of tremendous importance, is that of class control. The question is whether the churches, collectively or singly, are sufficiently free from class control so that they can engage in political activity in such a way as to effect change in society. (The question is considerably broader than whether the churches, especially the Protestant ones, reflect economic, racial, and ethnic lines. The answer, of course, is that, in general, they do.) In the most profound sense the question becomes whether the social classes of America are so accurately mirrored by particular denominations or groups of denominations that the latter can have no political movement except as reflections of the former.

The assumption underlying this set of questions is that social class is the most basic element of society and that each of the various institutions of society parrots the ideology associated with a particular class. In this view, it is inconceivable that in any meaningful sense the initiative for social change could come from the churches. For this school of economic determinism would allege, in one form or another, that the dynamic of history comes from the tensions generated among the classes, and that the most basic element of class is the relationship toward property and "the instruments of production." Stated in this fashion, the doctrine sounds distinctly Marxist, which it is. But the emphasis on classes and on conflict among classes has a very long history. In the United States it was popularized by James Madison, especially in several of his essays in *The Federalist*.[3]

In *The Federalist*, No. 10, Madison praised the proposed Constitution of the United States on the ground that it would tend to "break and control violence of faction." He asserted that faction is inevitable, since its "latent causes are sown in the nature of man." Faction is derived from "a zeal for different opinions," and from attachment to ambitious leaders and to parties. "But the most common and durable source of factions," he stated in a famous passage, "has been the various and unequal distribution of property."

He spelled out his position in these words:

> Those who hold and those who are without property have ever formed distinct interests in society. Those who are creditors, and those who are debtors, fall under a like discrimination. A landed interest, a manufacturing interest, a mercantile interest, a moneyed interest, with many lesser interests, grow

> up of necessity in civilized nations, and divide them into different classes, actuated by different sentiments and views. The regulation of these various and interfering interests forms the principal task of modern legislation, and involves the spirit of party and faction in the necessary and ordinary operations of the government.

The doctrine of class control explains both too much and too little. It is obvious that a very high correlation between upper-middle economic groups and the Republican party lends some substance to the sardonic jibe that the "United Presbyterian Church is the Republican party at prayer." But it is equally clear that such sarcasm (which supposedly originated with a seminary president!) is exaggerated and that it fails to explain in purely materialistic terms, for instance, why the same church should tax itself to help Cuban refugees who are not even Protestant. Most people would agree that class background has a good deal to do with denominational positions on some—though not all—occasions, but that class association with religious groups has not been sufficiently marked in practice to prevent churches from taking political and social positions which represent considerably more than simple reflections of class ideology.

It goes almost without saying—but it may be worth stating for the record—that no real believer would have any difficulty in disposing of the social-class-control argument. He probably would not convince a James Madison or a Karl Marx, but he would nevertheless assert unequivocally that the church, as a divinely ordained institution, is above class and race and nation. To the statement that this is a mere expression of faith, he would retort with justice that Marxism itself is also an expression of faith!

"Cultural Control"

A final external factor that affects the political potential of religious groups is cultural. In this sense "culture" does not mean "high-brow" or "arty" or "well-educated." It refers to the totality of the tools and beliefs that are available to a people at any one place and in any one epoch. "Culture" focuses upon the role of value-systems, for such systems are at the heart of any culture. The particular values present in any culture may be divided into those that are dominant and those that are subordinate, and they are often in conflict with each other. In contemporary America, a familiar example is the contrast between the majority-held concept of equality of opportunity and a minority-held concept that opportunity should be based on racial grounds.[4]

Outside of textbooks, critics of the American churches rarely deal with the profound questions of cultural determinism that are at the heart of many social anthropological studies. (For example, the assertion is frequently made that religion cannot transcend culture because it is merely a product of culture, which is man-made.) Instead, the critics understandably concentrate on specific values found in given regions and ask whether the churches and their members do not in fact merely reflect the dominant ideas. The most sophisticated of the critics refer to this phenomenon as "culture-religion," or sometimes as "tribal religion," terms that are obviously pejorative.

The most savage opponents of culture-religion are ardent churchmen who insist that the churches of America should provide the leadership in exposing social, economic, and political practices which are considered contrary to religious precept.[5] These churchmen become especially infuriated when religious symbolism is used overtly to bolster or maintain social institutions and customs that they deem immoral. Extreme cases are not hard to find: the playing of "The Old Rugged Cross" as background music at meetings of the Ku Klux Klan in Alabama, or the invoking of Biblical passages on Ham by Roman Catholic segregationists in Louisiana. It is easy enough to cite illustrations ad nauseam of the support given by Southern white Protestant churches and churchmen to the maintenance of a social system that keeps Negroes second-class citizens. What is less obvious but—to the critics—equally true is the reinforcement given by Northern churches through less flamboyant methods to the perpetuation of the American caste system. For whatever is familiar seems to many of us to be natural.

Social Change and the Churchmen

Even the most cursory acquaintanceship with the churches of America reveals that a large share of the criticism is valid. But would it not be strange were it otherwise? Given the fact that most Americans are, at least in a formal sense, church members, and given the fact that their local churches exist in all communities across the nation, is it at all unusual that the majority should share the views of the majority? It is simply not helpful to divide Americans into two camps—the religious and the nonreligious—and to assume that tension between the two forces ought to generate the steam for social pressures.

On the contrary, it is much more useful to divide the American public in terms of geography and size of constituency. One clue to social change, then, would be tension among religious groups. Another would be tension inside a particular group. Traditionally, historians have concentrated on the first type of situation, and this concentration has often led to the most pessimistic and blood-letting conclusions about the role of religion in politics. Agitation or tension inside large religious groups has often been overlooked by American historians especially, with the result that they have frequently been unaware of movements which transcend denominational lines. Prepared by their training to correlate denominationalism with specific programs of action, the historians have found it difficult to analyze or even understand such nondenominational phenomena as the Peace movement, the Prohibition movement, or the religious aspects of the Negro civil-rights movement of our time. It is not surprising that historians were slow to realize the relationship between "far-rightism" and fundamentalism.

If some historians generally have been disturbed by the discovery that religion is still a factor in American life, some social scientists have been upset at what they consider to be the inexcusable ineffectiveness of religion. C. Wright Mills, a leading social analyst, maintained that in times of crisis American religious leaders, for the most part, go along with and rubber-stamp any decision of the political elite.[6] There is considerable evidence to support Mills's sweeping charge, as the vigorous blessing given by clergymen to American (or Northern or Southern) arms in every war has attested.

Yet does the fact that most religious leaders, especially in times of crisis, identify themselves with the political elite mean that religion as such is too wedded to the dominant ideology to have a meaningful degree of independent political action? It is assumed by some sociologists of the Mills school that the United States is operated—perhaps at times in a helter-skelter fashion—by a kind of high-level central coordinating committee. (Mills assumes that the committee, or elite, is "irresponsible," but that is not relevant here.) This committee operates—figuratively—through a series of subcommittees—for example, on the military, on the schools, on labor, on business, on religion. Some difference of opinion is permitted—it is assumed—in ordinary times, but in times of great peril the central committee must present a united front to the world. When the ranks have been closed, at a sufficient distance they appear as one solid line. If this argument is valid, it means that free discussion and dissent are permitted as a luxury, not as a right, and only when nothing very important is at stake. It means that if the stakes are really high—the issues are war or peace, prosperity or depression, civil rights or civil repression—dissent will not be permitted by the ruling elite. Therefore no religious group could possibly take the initiative in challenging the political status quo.

In this form, the elitist thesis is simple, which may help to account for its popularity. When the Gauls are at the very gates of Rome, the Romans presumably drop all else to rally to the ramparts. Yet on very few occasions in American history has a crisis been of *this* type. Even during emergencies of the first magnitude, a relatively large degree of political maneuver has been permitted. Elections have been held on schedule, despite the existence of a state of war. So far as the churches have been concerned, their traditional freedoms have been maintained. In addition, even if the leading churchmen have rallied around the political elite, there have always been other churchmen who have continued to maintain their independent role. (Some of them may have gone to jail, but none, at least in recent times, has been shot.) There are limits to what even a totalitarian political elite can do to the churches, as witness the failure of Nazi Germany to destroy the Confessional Church. Whatever else the American political elite may be called, it cannot accurately be called totalitarian.

Elitists read history one way and democrats another, so that one cannot expect similar interpretations. But a democratic reading of American history can fully account for such religiously motivated activities in the political process as the Abolitionist movement, the settlement of Utopian colonies, the great Mormon experiment in Utah, the Peace movement, the drive for Prohibition, the tri-faith campaign launched in Chicago in January 1963 for equal rights for all citizens.

The question as to whether religion in America is or is not culture-bound—in the light of such considerations—becomes one of degree, not of absolutes. Americans who are church members share values with Americans who are not church members—this much is evident. What is less evident but equally true is that some church members have values (which may be good, bad, or indifferent) which are not universally accepted. What is also true is that the churches themselves are both repositories and breeding grounds of ideology. They can generate ideas, they can rearrange the emphasis on particular values in such a fashion as to win broad public acceptance for political change. The churches are not alone in their ability to do this, but under American conditions they have a base of operations that ought to make it easier for them to take the leadership than for some other institutions to do so.

THE NECESSARY INTERNAL CONDITIONS

Leadership

In order for the churches to exercise any measurable degree of influence on the political process they must fulfill certain conditions related to their internal lives. They must, in the first place, fulfill the obvious requirement of having leaders and followers. It is not enough to have only leaders! Size is important but it should not be overrated, for it often happens that relatively small groups—the Quakers, for example—are more influential in the political process than denominations many times larger. Both the caliber of leadership and the willingness of the great body of church members to be led are vital.

Tradition

Second, there is the denomination's tradition. It is relatively easy for churches in the Reformed family passionately to advocate social and political action. It is much more difficult for Lutheran groups to take any position that appears to involve interference with the activities of the state. For this reason, perhaps, the Lutheran churches in America, though strongly led and financed, have been relatively uninfluential in the political process. The Southern Baptist emphasis on separation of church and state—an emphasis which has been elevated almost to the level of a theological tenet—also often serves to curtail possible church-related political activity. This limitation is a consequence of the belief that some affairs of government are "off limits" to church groups, that the churches should not "interfere."

Finances

A third requirement is a firm financial base, not merely because it costs money for a church to engage in political action, but because a church had better be in a position to withstand financial reprisals if it is going to adopt statements or actions that may alienate some of its wealthy constituents. Many a minister and priest and rabbi learned this unpleasant lesson the hard way when well-to-do parishioners showed their hostility to the pastoral position on race relations by curtailing or even eliminating financial support. In principle, the higher the church judicatory, the better should be the ability of a church to repel a campaign against its coffers. In practice, the leading churches in the United States possess vast financial strength. They may often sound as though they were on the verge of bankruptcy, but such lamentations are not altogether to be taken literally. For the monetary needs of the churches are insatiable, and, in addition, it appears to be an ecclesiastical principle that church organizations should always be on the verge of financial overcommitment.[7]

A novel use was invented for the monetary power of American churches during the summer of 1963 in connection with the drive for greater Negro civil rights. Negro organizations had been insisting that certain state and city governments (in areas, to be sure, where the Negro vote was sizable) cancel present construction contracts or refuse to sign new contracts in construction projects where so few Negroes were employed as to imply discrimination. Several Roman Catholic dioceses and some national Protestant denominational agencies adopted a variation of this approach when they decreed that church construction in their jurisdictions must thenceforth be performed by work groups that were reasonably integrated.

Autonomy

A fourth condition, though related to group solidarity and to finance, is that of operating autonomy. This involves considerably more than leaving the churches alone. The Soviet Union leaves the churches alone—in the hope that they will wither and die. The idea of operating autonomy requires that the churches not only be able to manage their day-to-day internal affairs but also be able to plan and prepare for the future. Again, in contrast with the situation in the United States, the churches in the Soviet Union are not permitted to educate the young; they may not proselytize; they have been banned from the social-welfare area; they are severely limited in what they may print (the Bible has become a scarce commodity in the U.S.S.R.!). The number of seminaries is controlled and has, as would be expected, decreased savagely since the beginning of the Communist regime. The remaining Jewish synagogues operate under severe restrictions and Jewish cultural life is oppressed. In short, the picture of religion in the Soviet Union shows what can happen to church life and its institutions when operating autonomy is not permitted. In American society, the autonomy of the churches is not only protected, it is positively encouraged. Through schools and seminaries the churches have every chance to perpetuate themselves. In brief, the churches in America have a base from which they can attack and a refuge to which they can return.

Modern churches, like modern corporations, are multi-purpose agencies. The objective of the churches remains, no doubt, the salvation of the individual, but they embrace a wide variety of methods to achieve this goal. Of things to be accomplished, political action, as has been noted before, does not ordinarily rank at the top of the list. Paradoxically, the very diversification of their activities strengthens denominations when they decide to exercise an influence on the political stage. A large denomination, being engaged on several fronts and constantly in motion, presents an extraordinarily poor target for those who disapprove of its political activities. For this reason, the national governing body of a church can absorb more criticism for its political views than can a local parish church.

Detachment

It might seem that detachment is one quality absolutely dispensable for political success. In an individual, detachment is no doubt a liability. In an institution, however, it is to some degree indispensable. Here there is room for activism and for passivity; for colorful leaders and for detached observers. In this sense, detachment is more than a good thing in itself: it is a condition that a church must somewhere possess among its varied resources if it is to perform effectively a judgmental role in the political process.

A Note on Civil Disobedience

One of the oldest and most perplexing questions in political philosophy is under what conditions, if any, a citizen ought to feel morally justified in breaking the law. Normally the debate is carried on under conditions of academic calm, so that very strong argumentative positions can be asserted without any fear of adverse consequences. But there have been numerous cases in American history—most of which have gone unremembered because the participants were not especially well known—in which philosophical conviction has led to actual defiance of governmental authority.

One of the more famous incidents occurred when Henry Thoreau spent a night in jail after he had refused to pay a tax owed the Commonwealth of Massachusetts because that state tolerated the existence of slavery in some other states of the Union. In his celebrated essay "Civil Disobedience," Thoreau rests his case upon the conscience of the individual.[8] His argument is not explicitly Christian, but there is an honorable Christian, and especially Protestant, ancestry to his position on conscience.

Another dissident, Randolph Bourne, the hunchbacked genius who died of influenza at the age of thirty-two, castigated the modern nation-state with a vehemence that has not been matched before or since. He particularly hated the state because he considered it the cause of wars. In his *Unfinished Fragment on the State* (1918) Bourne savagely charged that war is "the health of the state." War crushes the individual, he said, but it results in a "vast sense of rejuvenescence" in the "significant classes."[9]

Just as a citizen's disobedience of civil law has been justified on the basis of moral standards, so a Christian's defiance of law has been founded upon religious obligation. There has been over the centuries a wide variety in attitudes toward civil authority as expressed by Christian thinkers and the groups they represented—as John C. Bennett has shown in his book *Christians and the State*.[10] Some, but by no means all, of the different historical schools of thought have had adherents in the United States.

There have been, for example, very few Christian anarchists in this country, and certainly none of the stature of the famous Russian, Count Leo Tolstoi. But there have been many Americans who have engaged in civil disobedience for religious reasons in the hope that their defiance of law would bring about some change in the law. In courting arrest, these protesters have been willing to gamble that subsequent publicity would create sufficient public indignation over the unjustness of the law so that the legislature would amend or repeal it.

In other cases the pattern is different in that there is no real expectation that defiance will actually result in changes in the law. The conviction and jailing of the Rev. Maurice McCrackin, the Presbyterian pastor of a joint Presbyterian-Episcopalian church in Cincinnati, is an example. The minister disapproved of the nation's armaments and defense programs, and to back up his disapproval he deducted that portion of his personal income tax he calculated would be devoted to such programs. As expected, the government took McCrackin to trial, the court found him guilty, and he was sentenced to prison. What was less expected occurred when the General Assembly of the United Presbyterian Church, acting as the highest appellate court of the denomination, upheld the action of the Presbytery of Cincinnati in deposing McCrackin on the ground that his defiance of civil authority was also an ecclesiastical offense.

Another type of civil disobedience often based on religious conviction occurs when persons refuse to take shelter during the course of air raid drills. Dorothy Day, editor of the *Catholic Worker*, has been a leader in this kind of demonstration in New York City and has been sent to jail as a result. There is no evidence to indicate that spending a month in a women's prison altered or even softened Miss Day's beliefs.

Civil disobedience could conceivably run a spectrum from open violence to passive resistance, but in fact the emphasis in America has been upon the latter. The technique of passive resistance is probably the method that an individual or a small group would ordinarily adopt. What chance do a few people have against the armed forces of law and order? It is only when the number of persons participating in a campaign of disobedience reaches sizable proportions that the use of nonpeaceful methods becomes a genuine possibility. As the proportion of active dissidents to the total population of an area increases so do the probabilities increase that some form of violence will be employed—all other things being equal. The caveat is crucial, for neither the forces of law and order nor the leaders of demonstrations ordinarily intend to let nature take its course. Both groups know perfectly well that the principal difference between an army and a mob is that one is disciplined and the other is not.

A notable characteristic of the great Negro civil-rights movement that began in the 1950's and gained momentum in the early 1960's was its reliance upon the technique of passive resistance. As applied by Negro students who violated municipal ordinances by demanding service at segregated lunch counters, the approved method called for the would-be diners to remain inactive even when taunted and pushed by provocateurs. In the case of actual arrest, Negro demonstrators were instructed by their leaders to submit peacefully to the police.

To use such tactics successfully required great discipline, which the Negro students and other Negro groups demonstrated that they amply possessed. What was also required was a rationale, a philosophy that justified nonviolence even under the most difficult circumstances. Ideally, such a philosophy would draw on the Negroes' deep belief in Christianity and at the same time offer a practical method of obtaining results.

It was the historic mission of the Rev. Martin Luther King to combine the theory and practice of nonviolent resistance to form a single consistent and hard-hitting doctrine. It must not be imagined that King read Thoreau one night and woke up the next morning with a fully developed theory of social action in his head. On the contrary, the maturation of King's ideas required several years and varying environments. During this process, he examined and rejected the theories of Marx and Lenin, and was impressed but not swayed by the pacifism of the Rev. A. J. Muste. Finally—as he describes in some detail in *Stride Toward Freedom*—he came into contact with Gandhi's writings and studied them with great care.[11] In Gandhi's emphasis on love and nonviolence he found "the method of social reform" he had been seeking.

The first large-scale test of the philosophy and practice of nonviolence, as developed by King, took place in Montgomery, Alabama, where he held his initial pastorate. Through the use of peaceful methods the Montgomery movement succeeded in desegregating the city's buses. From that time on, the doctrine of nonviolence gained widespread acceptance from Negroes, and its author became established as a national leader of the Negro community.

FROM LOCALISM TO INTERNATIONALIZATION

Prior to the Revolutionary War, the American religious scene, in broadest outline, was characterized by Anglicanism in the South, Congregationalism in New England, and Presbyterianism and Quakerism in the Middle Colonies. The Anglican Church was established throughout the South. In all of New England except Rhode Island, the Congregationalists were the established church. The Middle Colonies, alone of all the sections, subscribed to the principle of nonestablishment of religion. There were, of course, islands of Lutherans and Mennonites and Huguenots and others.

The most striking fact about the churches in the American colonies is that they were actually American outposts of European churches—especially of British Protestant churches. The point is so obvious that it is often overlooked. Over the decades the attitudes of some religious groups toward the central government in London changed sharply. For example, by the time of the Revolution, the New England Congregational clergy were on the point of sedition. As the conflict developed, Congregationalism and patriotism were closely identified, while, especially in the South, Anglicanism and Toryism tended to reinforce each other. The Anglicans paid a price for being on the wrong side of the war, for their church was disestablished at the war's end. The Congregational Church, in contrast, continued to hold a privileged position in most of New England into the 1820's.

Religion was an important ideological factor in setting the stage for and subsequently justifying revolutionary action against the British Crown. The disinclination to obey an unjust law because it supposedly conflicts with a higher (natural or divine) law is of ancient origin. In all probability the tendency to judge man-made law by such external standards will continue. The principle was very much in the minds of those ministers, Negro and white, who deliberately sought arrest in the great Negro civil-rights drive of the present decade in order to demonstrate and dramatize what they believed to be the inequity of certain statutes.

The state churches of the colonial era gave way to the voluntary churches of a pluralistic society following the end of the Revolutionary period. The process took time but, as has been noted, was completed early in the second decade of the nineteenth century. Thenceforth the process of converting the churches from the American outposts of European churches to independent churches in their own right proceeded at great speed. As large numbers of the population moved westward they did not always take their churches with them. For on the ever-moving frontier the churches found themselves on unfamiliar and extraordinarily difficult ground. The population of the frontier was no doubt "religious" but it was not, to use the apt if clumsy ecclesiastical expression, "churched."

The job of the leading denominations was therefore ready-made: to establish boards of national missions and to roll westward with the population. This they did, and as they did the Protestant churches more and more lost their distinctively European characteristics. Customs and attitudes peculiar to the United States began to become accepted as a legitimate part of the religious heritage and experience. Presbyterians, whose forebears in Scotland invented Scotch and drank it with zest, became Prohibitionists. The influence of the frontier spread across the land. Old denominations modified many of their traditional attitudes, generally in the direction of piety. What was even more significant was the rise and ascendancy of religious groups that displaced numerically the leading denominations of the colonial age. The Methodists and the Baptists, especially, came to typify the prevailing religion of America. Whole new denominations, for example, the Disciples, were created as the result of secessions. As the nineteenth century came to a close at least three religious groups were formed that had no counterparts in Europe. They were the Mormons, the Christian Scientists, and the Jehovah's Witnesses. As Littell has put it, the evolution was "from state church to pluralism," pluralism in the sense of bewildering diversity.[12]

A bird's-eye view of religious development during the nineteenth century would reveal one outstanding characteristic. This was the Americanization of religion, and, as a corollary, its increasing isolation from the religious forces of Europe.

At closer range the situation is less clear, for some religious groups—for example, the Lutheran ethnic churches—put up much more resistance to Americanization than did others. Catholicism might on the surface appear to be an exception to the over-all generalization. But when the internal tensions of nineteenth-century Catholicism in this country are taken into account—as Sperry and Olmstead[13] have done in their respective studies—it becomes apparent that Catholicism narrowly escaped being Americanized along with its Protestant rivals.

Immediately following the Revolutionary War it seemed quite possible that the Roman Catholic Church in America might become a layman's church, in the Protestant pattern. Of particular importance was the practice of lay trusteeship, which meant that lay members held title to church property. At the same time they attempted to manage parish affairs. A chronic shortage of priests also tended to strengthen the hand of the lay elements. To deal with these serious problems Rome permitted the American priests to choose their own bishop, with the result that they elected John Carroll, who became Bishop of Baltimore in 1790. Under Carroll steady advances were achieved in church organization, and by the time of his death in 1815 it was clear that Catholicism would survive.[14]

Nonetheless, the tone of American Catholicism disconcerted some Catholics. In particular there arose the question as to whether numerical and financial success had been obtained in part through too easy an association with customs and folkways that were more American than Christian. This question—which could have been and no doubt was asked of many denominations—was sufficiently important so that Pope Leo XIII in 1899 felt impelled to raise it in an Apostolic letter, *Testem Benevolentiae,* addressed to Cardinal Gibbons. The warning drew attention to the dangers of Americanism.[15]

From the point of view of religion and politics, the nineteenth century represents the high-water mark in the easy identification of religion with Americanism. It was possible to do this, without serious challenge, because America, religiously, was for the most part isolated from Europe. American religion quite understandably concentrated on winning the American West, and in the process severed its theological and organizational umbilical cord with its own past. The result was a mixed blessing, since the price of independence was an uncritical particularism, an unchallenged acceptance of the American way of life as the Christian way of life.

Under such conditions of myopia, it was not easy for the churches as churches to engage in politics or in political judgment in any significant and sustained fashion. There were church-led crusades, to be sure, and there were many cases of individual heroism—the Abolitionists and the Temperance fighters come readily to mind—but these were exceptions. Most churches and churchmen preferred to accept the prevailing cultural norms, which meant that in politics the status quo was accepted.

One of the reasons for the relative ineffectuality of religious efforts in politics, even up to the present time, has been regionalism. Most leading American denominations, including the Roman Catholics, are stronger in some regions than in others. The fact that religious strength is unevenly distributed clearly increases the difficulties for any one group to be effective in national politics. In this connection it is relevant to recall that of the great national Protestant denominations in existence prior to the Civil War only the Protestant Episcopal Church was not split into Northern and Southern denominations because of that war. The wounds have been slow to heal. In the case of the Presbyterians, there remain Northern and Southern churches, and in the case of the Methodists, the present North-South unity is often more apparent than real, especially if the dividing point is race. In addition, some denominations are almost entirely regional, such as the Southern Baptists.

The Roman Catholic Church and the three Jewish groups

should not in principle suffer from the disabilities that regionalism has historically inflicted upon Protestantism. In actual fact, it is much easier for Catholicism to present a united front on a question having political overtones than it is for Protestantism or Judaism. Judaism has so many fewer adherents than the other faiths that comparisons are difficult, but on a question which is of intense concern to all Jews—discrimination, for example—the Synagogue Council of America can and does obtain unanimity of views.

During the present century American Protestantism has in part succeeded in overcoming the divisiveness inherent in its own regional and denominational patterns. It has achieved this partial success through the creation of the modern conciliar movement, which includes the former Federal Council of Churches and its successor the present National Council of Churches (formed in 1950), and the several hundred related state and local councils of churches. It is true that the conciliar movement numbers among its cooperating communions various Orthodox churches, but the overwhelming program emphasis is Protestant.

The result of a long and complicated development is this: the nationalization of a very large part of the Protestant enterprise in America. Because several sizable (and mostly regional) denominations remain outside the conciliar movement, the nationalization is by no means complete. But for what have been called—and in a friendly sense—the old-line Protestant denominations, the process of nationalization through the conciliar movement has advanced spectacularly.

That this development has increased the political potential of Protestantism in the United States is beyond dispute. It has at the same time enhanced the freedom of action of Protestantism in the political arena by providing a broader base from which it can enter politics. Nationalization has also meant an enlargement of the perspective from which the Protestant churches can judge what goes on in all phases, including the political phase, of society. It is no longer necessary merely to reflect a parochial (or regional) viewpoint, or a compromise of parochial viewpoints. It is quite possible and feasible to adopt a national perspective even in the face of regional opposition. The increasing ability of the National Council of Churches to present nationally acceptable positions—even when such positions may stir up regional opposition—illustrates this point.

The next phase in the liberation of the churches of America from the shackling effects of nineteenth-century provincialism is already in progress. This phase is characterized by the internationalization of the churches, by their membership in international organizations and councils. In the case of the Roman Catholic Church, there was never in theory any question of its formal relationship to the Vatican. But here, as in other situations, the purely formal relationships may be deceptive. Many observers would maintain that in recent years—and especially since the Second Vatican Council—American Catholicism has been shedding an earlier isolationism and has accepted an increasing role in world-wide Catholicism.

Judaism, too, has been developing stronger international bonds. The rise of Zionism as an ideal and then as an attainable goal, the barbarities of the Nazis, the suppression of the synagogue by the Soviets have all served to increase the international perspective of American Jewry. Furthermore, formal cooperation between American and foreign Jewish organizations, at one time unusual, has now become commonplace.

The internationalization of Protestantism has also been advancing swiftly, though precisely how swiftly is difficult to judge. The movement has taken two forms—one confessional, the other conciliar. An example of a world-wide confessional or denominational organization is the World Presbyterian Alliance, organized in 1875, while the leading illustration of a conciliar organization is the World Council of Churches, formed as recently as 1948.

The continuing internationalization of the American Protestant churches has many aspects, including exchanges of personnel with non-American church bodies, mutual sponsorship of specific programs, and conferences of many types.

One by-product has been the travel education of top Protestant denominational officials, who since 1948 have logged millions of air and sea miles in fulfillment of their international commitments. At the same time, American Protestantism has benefited immensely from overseas churchmen. The horizons have been broadened immensely.

In terms of political effectiveness, the potential of the principal American churches has increased as they have outgrown their historic regionalism and become more national in scope and interest. By the same logic, their political potential should continue to grow as they become more and more internationalized. An ever-enlarging perspective—which is what internationalization in this sense means—should make it ever easier for the churches to perform effectively their judgmental role in politics.

CHAPTER THREE

Religious Diversity and Political Power

The modern concept of pluralism—in politics and in religion—lost popularity forty or fifty years ago, but in the last few years has regained its former status. Pluralism of course means more than one of anything, but like most words with a past, it carries with it specific associations. The essence of pluralism has remained the same over the centuries: a belief that the distribution of power among several groups has effects considerably superior to those resulting from the centralization of power in one group. In political and religious theory the concept of pluralism first appeared in medieval times, when it was employed both to justify and to defend the rights of the church against the feudal lords and barons. The idea was the antipode of the later concept of sovereignty, under which political power was concentrated in the hands of one authority.

The results of pluralism were supposed to be "superior" for everybody. Quite evidently, both a medieval theologian and a twentieth century guild socialist would have agreed that pluralism was not designed merely to protect what we would now call "special interests." Any resulting protection of particular interests would have been rationalized on the ground that this was the only feasible way to protect the interests of all. In addition to the Rousseau-like overtones inherent in this denial that the will of all could be obtained merely by counting individual preferences there is the further implication, stated explicitly by Lord Acton, that "power tends to corrupt and absolute power corrupts absolutely."

PLURALISM AS A MODERN DOCTRINE

Now these ideas, which are found in the thinking of twentieth-century pluralists, do not of themselves constitute a doctrine of modern pluralism. It remained for an assorted group of academicians, nearly all of whom were British, and all of whom distrusted the modern leviathan state, to develop a coherent theory. J. N. Figgis invoked pluralistic concepts to establish what he considered the community rights of the Church of England, and F. W. Maitland, drawing on the German Otto von Gierke, developed his noted theses on associations and on sovereignty.[1]

The idea of pluralism would probably not have left the universities had it not been for its appeal to various social reformers, especially the guild socialists. Such activist-intellectuals as G. D. H. Cole and Sidney and Beatrice Webb leaned heavily on the pluralist conception of the state as they developed their proposals for an economy characterized by self-governing guilds and cooperatives.[2] Such an economy was anchored firmly to the proposition that society could best be considered to consist of a number of groups or associations.

What does this mean for the state? Harold J. Laski, who was much taken with pluralism during his early writing years, had a ready answer in *Authority in the Modern State*.[3] He declared that the state is only one among a number of associations—bigger, but of the same *genus*. It is entitled to the obedience of a citizen only "insofar as it commands the citizen's conscience." On the one hand Laski advocated a sort of conditional anarchy, yet on the other he insisted that minorities had every moral right to exist.

Pluralism as a formal political doctrine offering a view of the state and of the citizen's place in it was seriously damaged by the First World War. Even academicians of febrile imagination found it difficult to reconcile the dreams of an individualistic society under a limited government with the nightmares of a collective society under a totally mobilized war government. Any residue of faith in the doctrine as the blueprint for an ideal society faded with the Great Depression and the rise of the Axis powers. It was then generally recognized —by Laski, among others—that it took force to countervail force.[4] In Britain, the guild socialists became old-fashioned socialists; they joined the Labour party. In the United States, they retreated back to the universities, where they taught intellectual and philosophical history.

Pluralism might have suffered the usual ideological fate of relics had not certain theologians stumbled on it and resuscitated it. What was revived was not, of course, guild socialism or anything resembling it. What was attractive to the theologians was a theory that allowed for a diversity of groups, in this case, religious associations, within a given society. Pluralism offered, at least potentially, a basis for rationalizing the diversity of religious groups actually found in the United States. Beyond this, pluralism, as applied to the churches, made it convenient to raise such questions as: What were the proper relationships among churches? What role ought the churches have toward government and the reverse? and What were the obligations of the parishioner as a citizen?

It is not possible to pinpoint the exact time and place when it became acceptable to refer to the diversity among churches in America as exemplifying "religious pluralism." Nonetheless, it is clear that the term had assumed the status of respectability by the mid-1950's, and probably earlier. As a term, its usefulness grew rapidly, first as a description of the religious situation in the country, and then as a theoretical and intellectual construct.

The new American nation, at the end of the Revolution, had a population of approximately three and one-half million persons. Of this number about 20,000 were Roman Catholics and some 6,000 were Jews.[5] It was therefore the custom to think of the United States as a "Christian nation," which under the circumstances meant a Protestant nation. There was certainly a good deal of religious diversity, that is, a division of the Protestant majority into innumerable denominations and sects. Yet it was taken for granted by nearly everyone that the diversity of sects did not in itself imply any religious disunity. It was believed that the United States was, for all practical purposes, one large Protestant religious community with more or less convenient subdivisions.

Roman Catholic, as well as Jewish and Orthodox, immigration in the nineteenth and early twentieth centuries changed the religious map of the United States drastically. As with many social changes, this religious shift took place much faster than did the social commentary which described it. It came therefore as a shock to many Protestants brought up in the belief that the country had and would always have a Protestant majority to learn after the Second World War that the country was no longer Protestant, that commentators were using such new expressions as "the post-Protestant era" and "post-Christian America." Commentators who used these and similar terms had a solid basis in fact. It will be recalled, for instance, that in 1961 Roman Catholics constituted 23.4 per cent of the total population, or 42,876,665 persons; Protestants 35.2 per cent, or 64,434,966 persons; and Jews, 2.9 per cent, or 5,365,000 persons.[6]

The country was, then, no longer Protestant, but it was also neither Catholic nor Jewish. A majority of the population claimed church membership, yet it was difficult to say in what sense the nation was "religious." From the historical perspective, the most striking comparison, of course, lay in the fact that a country which at one time was overwhelmingly Protestant in preference and outlook now had a Protestant minority. From another point of view, the outstanding fact was the religious disunity of the country. It has been contended by Will Herberg in his book *Protestant-Catholic-Jew* that contemporary Americans consider any one of the three principal faiths to be equally respectable, in the sense of public esteem and of proving one's Americanism. This is mainly because many people do not take their religion very seriously. The religion of America has become not Protestantism or

Catholicism or Judaism or some mixture of the three, but Americanism.[7]

These were the facts and conditions that made useful the term "religious pluralism," or, as employed by writers on religion, just "pluralism." As might have been expected, it has taken longer—in fact, the process is barely under way—to grasp the more theoretical implications of pluralism and to relate them to social and political phenomena. In this effort John Bennett of Union Theological Seminary and John Courtney Murray of Woodstock College have pioneered.[8] It is significant that two of the most distinguished contemporary American theologians, one Protestant and the other Catholic, each starting from a different theological base, have found the doctrine of pluralism valuable as they attempt to establish the relevance of their faiths to modern problems.

PLURALISM IN RELIGION

The diversity inside Protestantism that characterized the early years of the Republic and the pluralism of faiths that has replaced it as the outstanding contemporary aspect of religious organization in America have very strongly affected the religion-politics balance. The religious divisions, of both the former and the present type, have by their existence tilted the scales very strongly in favor of government. As a result, the influence of religion in politics has been far less than in those countries where religious diversity is either minimal or unknown. In countries where there is an official religion—as with Judaism in Israel, or Catholicism in Spain, or Mohammedanism in Pakistan, or Lutheranism in Finland—that religion expects and obtains considerations not usually accorded other faiths. In countries where one religious group is numerically dominant even though there is no state church—Catholicism in contemporary France is a good example—such a group quite understandably expects a preferential relationship with the state. The battle-cry of "one king, one church, one people," no matter how alien it may sound to Americans, has a long history. The religious diversity found in America is the exception, not the rule.

The anti-Federalist faction which insisted that a Bill of Rights be added to the Federal Constitution fully understood that divided religious forces might be at the mercy of aggressive politicians. The anti-Federalists successfully maintained that explicit prohibitions on Congressional action in the area of religion were necessary. The result, of course, was incorporation of this restriction into the First Amendment. It was only in this fashion that the potential imbalance of the religion-politics relationship in favor of government could be leveled off.

The First Amendment has therefore served as a constitutional brake upon the federal government, and its assimilation into the Fourteenth Amendment has similarly inhibited the states. In addition to holding the government at bay, the Constitution also accords religious organizations the same rights of association and agitation given other voluntary groups in American society. Despite these protections—one positive, one negative—religion in the United States has been far less effective in politics than in some other modern societies. The basic reason has been neither apathy nor ineptitude on the part of the churches but rather the presence of so many different churches.

Whether this situation is on the whole good or bad is a subjective matter. The objective consequences are plain enough. There cannot be an established, national church, nor can the states individually establish churches within their respective jurisdictions. There cannot be a great religiously based national political party in the manner of the Christian Democratic parties of Europe. Except for an occasional issue on which there is agreement, there cannot be concerted political action at the national level in the form of a single, continuing, across-the-board religious lobby. (It is, in fact, difficult to find a single issue on which the churches have united nationally. The frequently cited National Conference on Religion and Race, formed by agencies of the National Catholic Welfare Conference, the National Council of Churches, and the Synagogue Council of America, in January 1963 was perhaps the best example. Yet very many Protestant churches remained out of it.)

At the level of state and local government the advantage in favor of government often tends to be equalized, and in some cases the equilibrium may tilt in favor of the churches. A controlling factor—usually, *the* controlling factor—is the extent to which religious diversity is replaced by religious unity.

In any state of the Union there are constitutional and traditional limits to what a religious group may do in politics. Yet the potential influence of the Mormons in Utah, the Catholics in Rhode Island, or the Southern Baptists in Texas is immense. Influence, it seems, depends on concentration, and pressure need not always be explicitly exerted: it is enough to know that certain religious forces could be mobilized if there were a desire to do so. For there to be Mormon influence in Utah it is therefore not necessary for the Mormons to storm the state capitol and seize it by force. For the Congregationalists to be influential in the same state it might be necessary to march the Sunday school students, if they exist, through the streets of Salt Lake City.

Because religious groups are unevenly distributed, it often happens that a group which holds a minority in a particular state will form a majority or a plurality in the largest cities. Pennsylvania, with a Protestant majority, has Catholic majorities in Philadelphia and in Pittsburgh. If it is a very large majority—as is the case with the Catholics in Jersey City—it can obviously not be restrained by the remaining and minuscule religious groups. It is not difficult in such a situation for the majority religious group to have a profound influence on municipal politics.

The principle that the degree of religious diversity is a controlling factor in religious influence in politics is also apparent in those cities where there is a fairly balanced split among the faiths. In New York City, the ancient rule-of-thumb was to consider the population a third Jewish, a third Catholic, and a third Protestant. On this basis the politicians built a "balanced ticket," meaning that the slate of candidates put forth by any particular party should represent the three faiths and the principal ethnic groups in rough proportion to their numbers in the population. The formula left much to be desired since it assumed that all New Yorkers had some church relationship, which is far from true. It also, legitimately, added white and Negro Protestants to arrive at the supposed Protestant percentage. But in terms of *appointments* to office, the Protestants fared very poorly. Not in decades have a third of the judicial and high administrative posts been filled from their ranks. An alternative to the "proportional representation" approach was suggested by Negro civil-rights leaders during the 1963 demonstrations at New York City construction sites. This was to set arbitrarily a "quota" of jobs to be given to Negroes. If this approach is tried in the area of political appointments, it will be interesting to observe the reactions of the non-Negro party leadership!

As we have seen, the more local a majority the more likely it is to get its way—regardless of constitutions and statutes. A majority of Americans would probably support the proposition that prayer should be allowed in the public schools; yet they did not revolt when the Supreme Court declared that the Constitution forbade this practice. (It is true, of course, that a handful of states and some individual school districts in other states announced they would pay no attention to the ruling.) A majority of Pennsylvanians are not Roman Catholics; in all probability that majority is definitely opposed to the use of government funds of any sort to transport pupils to parochial schools. Finding itself caught between pressures to authorize and not to authorize local school districts to provide for such transportation at their option, the legislature engaged in heroic maneuvers to transfer responsibility from its own shoulders. In the summer of 1963 the Pennsylvania House of Representatives passed a bill permitting local school districts to supply transportation if they wished, and the Senate approved a constitutional amendment which, if eventually adopted, would remove any possible constitutional barriers to parochial school transportation with public—presumably local—funds. There was no rebellion on the horizon in 1963, and there will be none in fact if the proposals are eventually adopted as law. For if the legislature has its way, the field of battle will merely be transferred from the state to the locality. In particular school districts statewide losers are mathematically certain to be the ultimate victors. Those observers who would understand what is termed the "genius" of American politics would be well advised to study carefully how the Pennsylvania and other legislatures customarily handle questions on which public opinion is highly and emotionally divided.

At the municipal level there are fewer means of compromise. Ordinarily legislation is on a take-it-or-leave-it basis. A local minority based solely or mostly on religious affiliation is likely to remain so for a very long time. There is little opportunity for immediate reversal. It is perhaps this feeling of perpetual minority status that leads urban ministers to be so pessimistic when it comes to seeking social changes through politics. They could probably profit, in some cases, by reading history to see what action priests in similar circumstances took a hundred years ago in, say, Providence, Rhode Island.

The degree of religious diversity or unity affects with special acuteness legislation in the social welfare and educational area. The savage conflict in pluralistic Illinois between Protestants and Catholics over whether that state could give birth control information and devices to women on relief was characterized by a nearly total absence of *caritas.* Equally loud and bitter have been the disagreements over government assistance to Catholic schools.

Underlying much of the discussion on these subjects is the assumption that religious communities as such have certain rights and that the government has an obligation to protect and develop them. The assumption is fascinating for two reasons. First, it is a general repudiation of the doctrine that rights are invested in the individual citizen. In its most extreme form, it would demand for some citizens a privilege denied other citizens, for example, allowing a Mormon to have several wives at once. An opponent of these "Mormons' rights" would be labeled a bigot because he not only did not agree but asserted that the criminal law against bigamy should be enforced in the state of Utah.

A second cause for renewed interest in the theory is that it is related to pluralism. This concept, it will be recalled, held that minorities had every moral right to exist and ought to have every legal right to do so. The application of this principle in the United States is brilliantly illustrated by Indian reservations, where specific minorities are housed, fed, and encouraged to perpetuate themselves and their institutions.

It is the community, not the individual, that is considered the basic unit, and it is community rights that are being protected.

This view is the exact opposite of the melting pot theory, popularized to school children in the *Autobiography of Edward Bok*, and usually accepted by civics textbooks as the ideal end-result of citizenship education.

FATHER MURRAY ON PLURALISM

Father John Courtney Murray, of the Society of Jesus, professor of theology at Woodstock College, is one of the most distinguished of contemporary Catholic theologians. For nearly three decades he has commented incisively and elegantly on various aspects of American society, including the political, from the point of view of Roman Catholic theology. In the most traditional sense, he is not a systematic theologian, undoubtedly because he feels that the "system" he is so familiar with possesses fully developed principles. What he does, therefore, is to apply such principles to the specifics of American culture. In this process he has thrown considerable light upon American society, both for those who agree with and those who take issue with his theology. He has managed this by offering original analysis in a field often overgrown with stereotype and cliché.

In his book *We Hold These Truths* (1960) Father Murray has reprinted various articles and papers which, as the subtitle indicates, are "Catholic Reflections on the American Proposition." Some of what is said has an explicit bearing on the problems created by the existence of religious pluralism.

The basis of civil society, he declares, is "reason, or more exactly, that exercise of reason which is argument."[9] Civil unity, "qualified by amity, is the highest good of the civil multitude and the perfection of its civility."[10] "Argument" here means public discussion founded on reason and making use of reason in the "dialogue," or balanced exchange of views. The objective is to establish a consensus in the commonwealth. Barbarism is the opposite of "conversation," that is, it "is lack of reasonable conversation according to reasonable laws."[11] "Civility" is always difficult to achieve, but especially so in the United States, because of religious pluralism.

This state of affairs makes it difficult to carry on "civil discourse." It does this for two reasons: first, because in American society there is "no common universe of discourse"; secondly, because "we are aware that we not only hold different views but have become different kinds of men as we have lived our several histories."[12]

As a result, continues Father Murray, civic unity in the United States "is a thing of the surface."[13] Underneath it there is "a structure of war," and some four conspiracies are involved. (Father Murray defines a conspiracy as meaning common action for common ends.) They are Catholicism, Protestantism, Judaism, and secularism. The problem is "somehow to make the four great conspiracies among us conspire into one conspiracy that will be American society—civil, just, free, peaceful, one."[14]

Father Murray asks whether the problem can be solved and replies to his own question in these words: "My own expectations are modest and minimal. It seems to be the lesson of history that men are usually governed with little wisdom."[15] Thus peace is more an ideal than a realization, and religious unity, the highest spiritual good, encounters similar and grave difficulties. "Religious pluralism is against the will of God," declares Father Murray. Yet he adds in the next sentence: "But it is the human condition; it is written into the script of history."[16]

If religious unity is unlikely, what in actual practice can be done? The noted theologian makes two suggestions: "We could limit the warfare, and we could enlarge the dialogue."[17] The hope would be not to destroy pluralism but rather to destroy the "structure of war" which underlies it and replace that with "the more civilized structure of the dialogue."[18] In this way the "real pluralisms" would be clarified, "and amid the pluralism a unity would be discernible—the unity of an orderly conversation."[19] For example, given this kind of understanding, the author argues that it might be possible to discuss intelligently the problems of education in a religiously pluralistic society.[20]

Even from so brief an account of Father Murray's thinking, it becomes obvious at once that the Catholic theologian has raised the discussion of religious pluralism from the merely descriptive to a theoretical level. Father Murray finds no theological justification whatsoever for religious pluralism, yet he concedes that pluralism is likely to be present indefinitely. Under the circumstances he proposes to make the best of what to him is an unfortunate situation. He has no utopian solutions to suggest but rests his case on the intrinsic merits of his carefully reasoned exposition.

In contemporary Protestant and Jewish writings that touch on religious pluralism, it is difficult—perhaps impossible—to find analyses which satisfactorily make the transition from the purely factual to the theoretical. It is hard to understand why this should be so, since scores of books produced by Protestant and Jewish writers employ the phrase "religious pluralism." However, they are ordinarily merely describing a situation as they see it. Such discussion as is not altogether factual in nature generally turns into an analysis of the constitutional aspects of the doctrine of separation of church and state. This kind of analysis is more than helpful: it is essential in its proper sphere. But it does not even remotely come to grips with the kinds of problems that have been raised so pointedly by Father Murray.

Surely the questions posed by the Jesuit theologian deserve more attention from his Protestant and Jewish counterparts than has so far been accorded them. Perhaps the lack of treatment reflects basic inconsistencies in Protestant and Jewish theology, so that it is difficult to arrive at any statement which would command widespread acceptance. Or perhaps non-Catholic thinkers are too involved in the theological implications of mergers and new cooperative plans among their own groups to have the time or inclination to meet Father Murray on his own ground. But whatever the reasons—and persons close to the theological scene may know of additional ones—the failure of Protestants, especially, to develop a more coherent doctrine of pluralism may have consequences that range from the merely embarrassing to the seriously damaging.

The inability to hold their own in theoretical discussions would be embarrassing to Protestant delegates, but not irreparably harmful. Much more serious would be the failure of a dialogue, once begun, to proceed from the level of what Father Murray has termed "barbarism" to what he has called "argument." In any case, until they have succeeded in developing a comprehensive and relevant theology and philosophy of religious pluralism, Protestant participants in the dialogue are going to remain at a severe disadvantage vis-à-vis their Catholic counterparts.

A Note on "Subsidiarity"

The essence of politics is both the use and the distribution of power. For centuries theologians and church leaders have discussed how political power ought to be employed in contrast to the ways in which it is actually employed. A very few religious figures—Calvin is obviously one of them—have had the opportunity to try their hands at testing the theory. But not even Calvin, prolific though his writings were, had much to say about the distribution of power. Perhaps the reason is that this did not seem much of a problem in the small city-state of Geneva. But it is less easy to explain the relative silence of religious thinkers in larger countries, such as the United States.

An important contribution to this aspect of political philosophy took place in 1931 when Pope Pius XI in the encyclical *Quadragesimo Anno* formulated the "principle of subsidiarity." This concept was reaffirmed by Pope John XXIII in his encyclical letter *Mater et Magistra*, dated May 15, 1961.[21] Section 53 of the document begins by stressing the importance of the principle and then says that it is wrong for the state to undertake in the economy what the individual and private enterprise can accomplish. It continues by declaring that it is also "unjust and a gravely harmful disturbance of right order to turn over to a greater society of higher rank functions and services which can be performed by lesser bodies on a lower plane."[22] The reason for this is that a "social undertaking" ought to aid the "members of the body social, but never to destroy and absorb them."

It is remarkable that the idea of subsidiarity has not been more widely embraced in the United States, for it offers an excellent rationale for that decentralization of government which Americans so warmly profess. As applied to the United States, the doctrine very clearly means that a governmental function would in the first instance be entrusted to the local community government. If that unit of government could not effectively manage the matter, it would surrender the function to an agency of the state government. In turn, should the state government prove unable to deal with the question, as a very last resort the intervention of the federal government would be sought.

Public education in the United States has markedly followed the line of development recommended by the Pontiffs. The progression has in fact been from the local to the state level and there have been in recent years insistent demands for large-scale federal underwriting of the public-school system. Or, again, Congress conformed to the essence of subsidiarity when it established the Tennessee Valley Authority on a *regional* basis and accorded its management a large degree of operational autonomy. So useful a term as "subsidiarity" deserves a better fate than limited circulation in obscure theological journals. It ought to be made part of our working vocabulary of politics and government.

DENOMINATIONAL MERGERS

Religious diversity has complicated politics in the Western world only since Luther. Prior to that time religious diversity did not complicate political problems because all Christians owed allegiance to the Pope and the non-Christian minorities had little political power.

In those British colonies that later became the United States there existed from almost the beginning a wide diversity of Protestant groups, and their principal characteristics have been commented on previously. During the nineteenth century, as the country spilled westward, the centrifugal forces in American Protestantism were dominant. One religious secession followed another as the denominations and sects multiplied like amoebae. Almost always—and this fact is not sufficiently appreciated by historians—it was the right-wing groups, theologically speaking, that seceded from the main bodies. In this manner, for instance, the Disciples were formed from the Presbyterians, and the Churches of Christ were offshoots of the Disciples.

Had this tendency continued indefinitely, each Protestant might have constituted his own denomination. But the tendency did not, fortunately, continue. At some point in this century the centrifugal forces were overpowered by the centripetal pressures and on balance the trends toward merger became stronger than those toward secession. It was not just a question of the numbers of religious groups; it was more importantly a question of numbers of Protestants who were members of the merging denominations.

At first, the mergers took place in "families" of churches, for example, the great Methodist merger in the late 1930's or the series of Lutheran mergers during the 1950's and 1960's. The creation of the United Church of Christ brought together two denominations with totally different ethnic and governmental backgrounds as the Evangelical and Reformed Church joined with the Congregationalists.

The most dramatic plea for Protestant unity in modern times was delivered on December 4, 1960, at Grace Cathedral, San Francisco, immediately prior to the convocation of the triennial General Assembly of the National Council of Churches. The Rev. Dr. Eugene Carson Blake, chief administrative officer of the United Presbyterian Church and past president of the National Council of Churches, had been invited by his host, the Right Rev. James A. Pike, Bishop of California, to deliver the morning sermon. The cathedral was jammed to capacity, since advance information published by the press had indicated something of unusual importance was to be said. Dr. Blake did not disappoint his audience. He called for negotiations to bring about the merger of the United Presbyterian Church, the Episcopal Church, the Methodist Church, and the United Church of Christ. He was followed by Bishop Pike who, in a carefully phrased statement, associated himself with the bold suggestions of his guest speaker.

The Blake-Pike proposal for church unity will if successful bring together at least twenty million Protestants. As the negotiations envisaged by Dr. Blake and Bishop Pike eventually got under way, their base was enlarged to include additional denominations. It is easy to appreciate the excitement that the church unity proposal engendered and to see why the country's religion reporters voted it the "outstanding religious story of the year."[23]

At least three important political consequences would be expected to ensue from the contemplated Protestant merger. A first effect would be the strengthening generally of middle-of-the-road politics and the relative weakening of the fundamentalist, right wing of Protestantism. For not only is the process of merging in itself an act of moderation, but the denominations invited to merge are themselves committed to a policy of moderate and responsible social action. By uniting the moderates the act of union ought to isolate those radicals of the right who combine religious fundamentalism and reactionary politics.

A second result of large-scale Protestant union would be to challenge the usefulness for political action of the whole conciliar movement as it operates inside the United States. At the present time, the National Council of Churches, as the cooperative agency of the leading denominations, has been assigned the role of acting as the avant-garde in social and political action. In this respect it has inherited the actionist tendencies of its principal predecessor, the Federal Council of Churches.

A Protestantism united along the lines of the Blake-Pike proposal would not need the conciliar movement as it now exists. However that movement evolved, if it survived at all, it would undoubtedly be largely divorced from social and political action. For it is inconceivable that the new and vast united church would delegate matters of a political import to an agency whose usefulness had atrophied. On the contrary, the new church would directly handle and manage such questions as political representation, endorsement of legislation, and the influencing of public opinion.

It is the final implication of a vast Protestant merger that exhilarates some observers and worries others. For persons who believe that Protestantism has necessarily shunned its social responsibilities because of meaningless divisions and squabbles, the envisaged church union opens up an almost unlimited potential for united and responsible political and social advances. Such persons believe that a church with twenty million members would inevitably attract most other Protestants and millions of non-church members to its leadership. Under these circumstances, the political influence of Protestantism could be increased many-fold.

There are several reasons why some people are less than enthusiastic about the proposed gigantic Protestant merger, and a few of these reasons have to do with politics in the broadest sense. In some states and in some whole regions of the country the united church would have, for all practical purposes, a religious monopoly. It is quite possible that such a church might exercise its political influence with restraint and tolerance. But there is always the danger that a religious body in a monopolistic situation might be tempted to throw restraint to the winds and impose its views through legislation on the public in general. Concomitantly, there is the prospect of militant anticlericalism, something that has thus far been rare on the American scene.

It should be noted that suspicions of the proposed merger because of fear of its possible adverse effects upon the body politic are not limited to rabid anticlericals, professed agnostics, and militant civil libertarians. There is deeply rooted in American Protestantism itself the belief that bigness leads to power, and that all power—ecclesiastical as well as political—needs to be checked. In rebuttal, proponents of the merger thesis would argue that this was hardly the real issue even if they agreed with the general proposition. A united Protestantism is needed, they would say, in order to offset or check united Catholicism. Only by uniting, they would contend, can Protestantism be in a position to command respect and to make its potential influence felt in American life, including American political life.

RELIGIOUS UNITY AND POLITICS

Come what will, there has been launched in American Protestantism a movement which if successful will help solve the problem of religious diversity by bringing together into organic unity Protestant elements which have been separate.[24] As has been observed, any degree of achievement in this direction is bound to have political consequences, although it is only fair to add that there is no precise agreement as to what those consequences might be.

The creation of Protestant unity, or a high degree of it, leaves unresolved the historic problem of religious pluralism, since the Protestant-Catholic-Jewish trichotomy would still exist. Yet most of that problem would be solved if the Protestant and Catholic churches were to be re-united as they were before there was any Reformation. The Second Vatican Council did much to spur hopes that "in the long run"—a rather conveniently distant time—such a unity of Christendom could be achieved. (It is usually assumed, in discussions of this sort, that Orthodoxy would join the other two groups in any unification effort.)

As recently as twenty years ago a Protestant minister who publicly suggested that Rome and Geneva ought to unite would undoubtedly have been relieved of his pastoral duties. It is a sign of the times that such suggestions have now become commonplace on the part of the Protestant ministry. At the same time the traditional isolationism of the Catholic clergy has been dissolving in a rising wave of inter-faith dialogues and seminars. There have even been cooperative efforts to achieve common community goals—something unheard of a decade or two ago.

An indication of better relations is the virtual elimination from the conversation of non-Catholics of the cliché: "I have nothing against Catholicism as a religion. It is only its political power I dislike." That political power was in fact the intended target of such an observation seems less likely than that it was a smoke screen, for the obvious thought being expressed is fear of Catholicism. Not only has this element of fear been diminishing but the pendulum has swung in the other direction, as the election of John F. Kennedy to the Presidency in 1960 attested. A typical comment was that of a well-known Presbyterian minister who observed that the Second Vatican Council had accepted so much of the essence of Protestantism that he wondered if there were any point to maintaining Protestantism as a separate branch of Christendom.[25]

There does seem to be a strong interest in achieving Christian unity in the United States. Suppose that most of the Protestant churches and the Roman Catholic Church in the United States should eventually merge. Clearly, the effects would be monumental, and the political results would be incalculable. Depending on one's point of view, there would be new opportunities for the churches or new difficulties, but in any event new challenges.

CHAPTER FOUR

Accommodation and Conflict in Church-State Relations

The churches and the state constantly woo the same personality—the public. In this contest the third party is not necessarily passive. For purposes of this analysis, however, we shall concentrate on the relationships between the churches and the state and by-pass the active role of the people, that is, public opinion, parties, and interest groups. The following is an analysis of the impact of church and state on each other.

To a casual reader of our daily newspapers, occasional statements by church leaders and occasional references to religion by political leaders may seem to be devoid of pattern, and possibly of meaning. The assumption of this chapter is that church-state relationships, when viewed in terms of current group theory, make a good deal more sense than our casual newspaper reader might imagine.[1] It is not heretical to suppose that the same principles of group conflict and of group accommodation that apply, say, to labor and management situations, may also be of help in analyzing church-state relations.

Viewed in this perspective, the churches are social organizations. Of course, they are and claim to be a good deal more than that. But they are, in fact, social organizations. They seek to control people, and they are both actual and potential interest groups.

Government may be one or many social organizations, depending upon the issue under consideration. Government also is and claims to be more than just any ordinary social organization. But like other groups, government attempts social control. That is a large part of its job.

A TYPOLOGY OF CHURCH-STATE RELATIONS

There is an area of overlap, in which the claims of churches and of the state may be and often are in conflict. If one were to picture the state as one circle, and the churches as an adjacent circle, the two circles would overlap considerably, mainly where they both issue positive and sometimes conflicting directives. In this process, neither side ordinarily wins hands down. Sometimes the state gives in, at other times the church. But at all times there is some degree of tension in the situation. Happily, we have not had in this country any momentous church-state showdowns of the sort that have occurred repeatedly in France. However, it is suggested that seven types of situations arise often enough in the relationship between church and state so that they may be clearly identified. The problem before us now is to examine in some detail specific examples of each general situation.

Church and State Activities Not Overlapping

There is little conflict in the area that is defined generally by the constitutional provision for free exercise of religion. Neither federal nor state governments concern themselves in our time with the liturgy, ritual, or contents, of preaching in particular churches. Provided that preachers do not incite their congregations to commit illegal acts or in some other way to break the law, they are free to preach what they please. This remains the case whatever laymen may or may not think of particular statements issued by preachers or by church bodies.

When one church sues another over control of property—as has happened often—an agency of government, the judiciary, of course acts as referee. The rendering of such a service by government does not pose any issue of church-state relations, and therefore may be included among those activities where church and state activities do not overlap.

In the other six situations, which we shall now consider, some measure of conflict is involved. The illustrations are drawn from recent or fairly recent American history.

The Government Trying to Use the Churches

Late in the Presidential campaign of 1960 Senator Kennedy advanced the general idea of a "peace corps." While he was not very specific, he said enough to excite the imaginations of thousands of people, especially those of college age or recent graduates. A reservoir of youthful idealism existed, much to the surprise of older generations.

After Mr. Kennedy won the election, it became necessary for him to carry out the peace corps idea. He appointed Robert Sargent Shriver, Jr., as head of the Corps, and Mr. Shriver shopped around for specific suggestions. It had apparently been the original hope that the universities and the churches would serve as the principal channels for recruitment of the corpsmen. In addition, it was hoped that the universities and the churches would offer to cooperate with the Peace Corps as it undertook projects in countries requesting assistance.

The colleges responded positively. Deans of students throughout the country explored with students the pros and cons of signing up for the Corps. Several universities offered their facilities for various overseas projects. Experts in "overseamanship," such as those at the Maxwell Graduate School at Syracuse University, offered specific advice to the management of the Corps.

But the Protestant churches found themselves in a dilemma, which took a year to resolve. On the one hand, they could only applaud the idea that young Americans should serve overseas to aid people in less developed countries. On the other hand, in a very real sense, they felt they could not place their facilities overseas at the disposal of the United States government. On this issue the Corps decreed, after some sharp prodding from secularists, that its workers could not engage in any form of religious proselytizing. The corpsmen were to enjoy, of course, the freedom to carry on their own individual religious practices. But they were specifically forbidden to serve as quasi-missionaries. The churches argued that they were overseas primarily to spread the Gospel, and only secondarily to carry on good works. There was a second issue: Was it proper, the churches wondered, for them to act in any sense as agents of the American government?

Some churchmen also speculated that the Peace Corps might drain off a large number of young men and women who might otherwise have become missionaries for the overseas boards of the churches. After all, at any given time, the number of persons willing to serve abroad at low pay under primitive conditions is strictly limited. For most young persons desiring careers overseas the more attractive paths are the diplomatic service, the armed forces, or business. The churches and the Peace Corps would, some churchmen felt, have to compete for the hard core of dedicated idealists and visionaries.

The Protestant churches could not solve the problem simply by refusing to let their facilities be utilized by the government, and they knew it. Nor did they wish to be accused of acting only on behalf of their own interests. After almost a year's hesitation, the churches, through their cooperative agency, the National Council of Churches, took a significant and positive step. They established inside the Council a Peace Corps office to meet a rising interest in and increasing demand for information from the Protestant denominations.

On January 2, 1962, the new office was opened, with the Rev. C. Frederick Stoerker as its head. The purpose of the office was announced as "to fulfill a liaison and educational function between the churches and the Peace Corps." Mr. Stoerker, in an interview, declared that his office would have three main functions. It would supply information about the Peace Corps to the churches, and inform the Peace Corps about the churches. "In addition," he said, "we will deal directly with Church young people interested in service in the Peace Corps who view this as an opportunity to express Christian vocation."[2]

Mr. Stoerker would continue his duties as head of the Commission on Ecumenical Voluntary Service Projects of the Council's National Student Christian Federation. The announcement continued: "In operation since 1947, the Commission serves as a kind of church Peace Corps. In 1961 it sent 250 American young people to 37 countries to participate in work projects ranging from rehabilitating slums to building churches."[3]

The Roman Catholic Church in the United States had from the start taken a position directly opposite to that eventually adopted by their Protestant brethren. It was made known that Catholic cooperation overseas could be counted on. When the Peace Corps did ultimately announce that it would make no contracts with religious agencies, the Roman Catholic reaction, while restrained, was highly critical. In January 1962, at its meeting in Atlantic City, the National Lutheran Council, a cooperative instrument of Lutheran communions with about five million members, voted an action almost identical in spirit with that taken by the National Council of Churches.

It may be wondered why the government was so eager, for many months, to enlist not only the moral support but the active participation overseas of both Protestant and Catholic churches. Very simply, the answer is this: the churches have had the greatest experience of any agencies operating overseas in dealing with people in less developed countries on a person-to-person basis.

In effect, the Protestant position forced the Peace Corps to rule against making contracts with any church groups. As we have noted, this meant overriding the Roman Catholic position. It would not have been politically possible for the government to sign contracts only with the Catholics. Mr. Shriver solved the problem by ruling that contracts would be made only with secular organizations. In so doing, he necessarily lost a great deal of potential support that he had originally counted on.

The purpose of the above observations is neither to praise nor to condemn the Peace Corps or the churches. Rather the objective has been to illustrate a situation in which the government wanted to enlist a certain type of support from the largest religious group in the country, the Protestants, and was turned down. In this case, the objectives of government and of the Protestant churches were not compatible. Hence a formula of liaison, not of active partnership, was worked out.

The Churches Trying to Use the Government

The most notable illustration of successful mobilization of church members to change national law was of course the passage of the Eighteenth Amendment. It remains the most dramatic example of the power of church groups, in this case Protestant, to use the device of law to try to impose social controls over the behavior of the total population.

Yet there are many other areas of life in which church groups attempt to affect legislation. They have every right to do so. The ethical problem arises when the effort is, or seems to be, to impose by law standards held by one group on all other groups in the population. For example, who is to say whether bingo is or is not a sin and should be outlawed on the ground that it is a social menace? There is an honest difference of opinion on this question between most Catholic spokesmen and most Protestant spokesmen.

The official statement of the New York State Council of Churches says: "Gambling is a moral and social evil. It defeats true benevolence, promotes the harmful philosophy of getting something for nothing and undermines our economic order. Ultimately it leads to social demoralization and the breakdown of personal integrity."[4] The statement ends with a call for the repeal of the Bingo Amendment to Article I, Section 9, of the New York State Constitution. This amendment, generally opposed by official Protestant bodies, was carried by a surprisingly high percentage of the voters during a referendum in 1957. It was noted by observers that even in heavily Protestant up-state New York towns, the proposed amendment to legalize bingo for the benefit of religious, fraternal, benevolent, and government groups did extremely well. Apparently, some Protestants were prepared to place a higher value on raising income for volunteer firemen's associations and other groups than they were on observing the strictures of Protestant leaders. In heavily Roman Catholic areas of the state the proposed amendment carried with no trouble.

A parallel situation arises, of course, when the Roman Catholic Church, through one of its bodies, attempts to have its moral concepts put into law and enforced on all citizens. The question of whether New York City's municipal hospitals could or could not answer questions on birth control and supply contraceptive devices to patients is one illustration. Newspaper inquiries into the practices of the municipal hospitals revealed that over the years hospital authorities in their regulations and procedures had largely adopted Roman Catholic moral teachings as the key criteria in deciding how to handle patients' requests concerning birth control. As a result, the hospitals refused to give out the information or devices. After an extensive investigation, the regulations were changed so that doctors in municipal hospitals could dispense both information and devices to patients.

The anachronistic birth-control statutes of Massachusetts and of Connecticut merely illustrate the same type of problem on a much larger scale. So far, Catholic forces have been strong enough to defeat all efforts at repeal. Anyone wishing to can no doubt think of similar instances where a religious group has tried to force its own concepts, through law or by economic means, upon the general public. Enough has been said to develop the kind of situation we have in mind.

Church and State Cooperating to Achieve Mutually Compatible Ends

A good example of this situation comes from the relationships between the United States government and Church World Service. Church World Service (or CWS) is the overseas relief and rehabilitation arm of the National Council of Churches. It was formed in 1946. Most of the larger Protestant and Orthodox communions in the United States are members of CWS. In addition, several large denominations which are not members, such as the Southern Baptists and the Missouri Synod Lutherans, informally cooperate with CWS.

It is fair to say, then, that CWS is an agency of the overwhelming majority of Protestant and Orthodox churches.

The scope of CWS activity is impressive, as some over-all statistics indicate. The income contributed by the churches, individuals, corporations, and foundations amounted in 1960 to about $3,900,000. Refunds for ocean freight (which will be explained later) came to about $4,300,000. Together with miscellaneous other receipts the total cash income was $8,391,355. Using this financial base as its support, CWS was able to distribute during 1960 some 298,605,262 pounds of food, clothing, and other material valued at $25,623,373.[5] This distribution was world-wide and literally affected millions of people.

What has all this got to do with the question of church-state relationships? Simply this: a large part of the CWS program depends on active cooperation on the part of the government. To be more specific, the government, under Title III of Public Law 480, makes available to CWS surplus commodities. These commodities are then shipped by CWS to distribution centers around the globe. The International Cooperation Administration subsequently reimburses CWS for ocean freight bills incurred in shipping the commodities. During 1960, wheat, wheat flour, corn, cornmeal, powdered skim milk, and rice were given by the Department of Agriculture to CWS. The value of these commodities was placed at $17,584,807, and the net pounds reached the staggering figure of 287,491,644. CWS used during 1960 nearly 100 steamship lines to transport materials overseas. These materials included clothing and other items which were not reimbursable by the government, but government reimbursement—for the commodities just mentioned—came to $4,323,177. It might be noted in passing that CWS was able to ship 400 pounds per dollar, which should cheer those people who contribute to it from local congregations through the annual drive known as "One Great Hour of Sharing."

CWS has also been extremely active in cooperating with the government through its immigration services program. In 1960, CWS met 202 ocean liners and 298 transoceanic air flights to welcome 6,745 homeless refugees into the American

Protestant community. From the end of the Second World War to April of 1960, CWS and the denominations working with it sponsored the immigration to this country of 111,643 persons. This sponsorship was made possible, of course, by a series of United States statutes. In addition, CWS must often work out a cooperative arrangement with a foreign government. For example, the program designed to assist Dutch Indonesian refugees involved negotiations between CWS and the Netherlands Emigration Service.

There are other areas of activity where CWS and the United States and other governments enter into a cooperative relationship. But enough has been said to demonstrate that the overseas commodity program and the immigration program involve a close partnership between agencies of the state and an agency of the churches. A good part of the CWS operation, such as the shipping of clothing and medicines overseas, does not depend on the government for support. But beyond any shadow of a doubt acquisition of surplus foods and the shipping of them overseas could not occur on a sizable scale unless the government had recognized CWS as a voluntary agency registered for this purpose. Similarly, the immigration and resettlement programs represent the most intensive kind of church-state cooperation.

One further consideration should be noted: CWS must carry on its work within some framework of American foreign policy. Happily, in this respect, the government has been broad-minded. But the government could easily force CWS to stop relief to, say, Poland, Yugoslavia, and Ghana. By permitting American shipments to be made through a voluntary agency to these and other countries, the State Department is obviously hoping to do indirectly what it could not do directly. From the point of view of CWS this does not matter, for its only reason for existence is to ship foods and materials to individuals who are in need.

Catholic Relief Services, a unit of the National Catholic Welfare Conference, is analogous to CWS, as is the United Jewish Appeal, a division of the Synagogue Council of America. The three relief agencies cooperate in many ways.

Economic Interests Using the Churches' Influence on the Government for Economic Ends

No doubt the classic example of economically interested people posing as concerned churchmen pursuing church objectives comes from that fount of so much experience—Prohibition. While the situation could have been and was repeated in a number of states, it is instructive to consider Kansas during the time prior to the Second World War when it still maintained Prohibition (as was its right) despite the repeal nationally of the Eighteenth Amendment.

The Women's Christian Temperance Union had for many years been one of the more active Protestant lay organizations. It had been notably successful in keeping Kansas "dry." It rarely lacked for funds or organizational talent. Yet it might have surprised the ladies to learn that one large source of WCTU revenue was the bootlegging interests. It had been arranged that Kansas was divided by the bootleggers into spheres of interest; each particular sphere constituted a virtual monopoly. It was the custom of the bootleggers, in order to maintain this monopoly and charge what prices the traffic would bear, to contribute handsomely to the campaigns of the "dry" organizations, including the WCTU. When Kansas finally amended its constitution and repealed the state-wide prohibition laws, the bootleggers, facing competition for the first time in their lives, found themselves ill-prepared to convert to honest businessmen and compete on the free market. The WCTU, however, continued its vigorous campaign to have the repeal amendment repealed.

A similar situation existed for many years in Oklahoma. When the voters amended the constitution and provided that the legislature could regulate liquor distribution through state law, they could not have foreseen one result of living in dry territory: the prices of liquor went up under state control over what they had been when the bootleggers had a monopoly!

Another example of the occasional confusion between religious and economic motives comes from the never-never land of Sunday closing laws. These laws go far back in colonial history, and their original purpose was beyond question to sanctify

Sunday. Gradually these laws fell into disrepute. Over the decades where the laws themselves were not drastically changed, for example, in Vermont and in Pennsylvania, they were rarely literally enforced.

Three developments following the Second World War revived the question of Sunday closing laws. In the first place, a by-product of the religious revival was a renewed effort to enforce and to redefine state Sunday observance laws. The general idea was to eliminate all business transactions on Sunday except those that were necessary. For example, department stores would be closed but pharmacies were expected to remain open.

A second development and a contradictory one, was the drastic changes that American families were making in their shopping habits. Especially in the increasingly motorized suburbs, Americans more and more were making purchases of major household items and clothing on Sundays.

A third development was the new public support shown by the Catholic clergy for the enforcement of the Sunday closing laws. In this fashion a movement strongly backed for many years by the Lord's Day Alliance, a Protestant organization, received vigorous reinforcement. In addition, it should be remembered that state and local councils of Protestant churches almost always support state and city Sunday closing laws. This is so even when the great national denominations have been silent, as they almost must be where the diversity is too staggering for a general statement to carry much weight locally.

This generally uneven picture—of sporadic enforcement of laws that many consumers did not want to be enforced—came into sharper focus when the Supreme Court in May 1961 upheld the constitutionality of several state Sunday closing laws.[6] Public interest in the decisions was remarkably, and understandably, high.

We could list the reactions state by state, but what happened in New Jersey amply illustrates the general confusion. The legislature of that state, stung by criticisms from both rival camps, got off the spot by passing a law permitting the citizens to decide for themselves whether they wanted certain

Sunday closing provisions or not. The referendum was conducted on a county-by-county basis. Of the thirteen most populous counties, some twelve adopted the provisions. (What the provisions do or do not mean will be the subject of litigation for years to come!)

Who were the contestants in the referendum? Superficially, the contest could have been viewed as one between all the Protestants, Catholics, and liberal Jews against all the Seventh-day Adventists, Orthodox Jews, and atheists. The battle should have been, but was not, completely one-sided. It is submitted that the issues were basically economic, involving primarily sellers and buyers. It is further contended that most persons voted as sellers or buyers and not as members of particular religious groups. There is no other way to explain the closeness in the voting.

In Bergen County, New Jersey, for example, the issue between two types of sellers was quite clear. The large discount houses, strung along the highways, had been tremendously successful in wooing the buying public to spend its money with them on Sundays. Even more, this Sunday shopping had tended to become family shopping. On these same Sundays the smaller stores in the towns and boroughs tended to remain closed, as in the past. The result was the transfer of a substantial amount of business from the closed-down town stores to the wide-open highway discount houses.

A third and very important element in the struggle was, of course, the consuming public. It is apparently impossible to obtain reliable statistics as to the degree to which the consuming public preferred Sunday to other-day shopping. But ordinary observation confirms at least the general point that a substantial portion of the hard-working men and women of Bergen County preferred to rest from their week's labors on Saturday and to do their serious heavy shopping on Sunday. This change in shopping habits appears to have affected a sizable percentage of the entire American population, in those places where Sunday shopping for general merchandise is permitted.

To many persons, what the churches had been saying must

have seemed irrelevant, or self-seeking, or a plot to deprive them of a chance to combine a day of leisure with an opportunity to purchase. From the point of view of many merchants, it is desirable to encourage in the minds of customers the idea that shopping may be considered a legitimate way to spend leisure time.

The above observations on the struggle for Sunday closing laws are made to illustrate the point that often what seem to be religious considerations are not so in fact. The small shopkeepers in Bergen County are presumably no more nor less religion-minded than the men who manage and work in the giant discount houses and shopping centers. Church statistics indicate a reasonable degree of religious affiliation throughout the county, which would mean that the general public, or consuming public, considers itself relatively religious. The point is that the arguments advanced in the name of religion carried considerably less weight than the arguments advanced in the name of economics. In a sense, the churches had become unwitting participants in what was basically an economic contest. It is a contest that will continue.

The Church Defying the Government

With some exceptions then—such as the historic outlawing of polygamy in Utah or possibly the current cases involving state aid to parochial schools—the relationship between government and the bigger churches has been placid enough. We have to go outside the traditional patterns of church behavior to find instances where religious groups in recent times have declared all-out war on government.

As would perhaps be suspected, the best illustrations come from the sect known as Jehovah's Witnesses. The group has several characteristics that distinguish it from the traditional churches. For instance, every member considers himself a minister and, as such, able to spread the Gospel. Emphasis is placed on the Second Coming of Christ, which is believed to be imminent. All organized religion and all organized government are believed to be the works of Satan. Organized religion is bitterly attacked by the Witnesses, while there is a tendency to treat government less seriously on the ground that it is illusory and ephemeral. In any event, the Witnesses are not militant anarchists.

They have been extremely sharp in their spoken and written criticisms of the organized churches, however. They have distributed their literature from house to house and have broadcast from sound trucks. Very often community resentment has been intense, and communities have used numerous legal devices to restrict the activities of the sect.

For their part, the Witnesses have fought all attempts to restrict their activities by law with fanatic zeal, and have won a majority of the more than twenty cases they have fought before the Supreme Court. Whatever one may think of the theology of Jehovah's Witnesses, the fact is clear that this sect almost single-handedly forced the Supreme Court to develop a consistent constitutional doctrine relating to freedom of religion.

Let us briefly review some of the cases. In the first case, *Lovell* v. *Griffin* (303 U.S. 444; 1938), it was held that a municipal ordinance prohibiting the distribution of all literature within the city without the written consent of the city manager was censorship and therefore a denial of due process of law. The Witnesses, of course, had circulated tracts without obtaining permission and thereby challenged the law. In subsequent challenges the finer points of doctrine were worked out by the Court. For instance, in *Cantwell* v. *Connecticut* (310 U.S. 296; 1940), the Court declared unconstitutional a state law that required prior approval from the secretary of the public welfare council before religious literature could be distributed. The Court also held that Cantwell could not be punished for a breach of the peace for playing phonograph records on the street, even though the records were severely offensive to those who heard them. The Court held that this right is part of religious liberty protected by the Constitution.

Another phase of the Witnesses' cases concerned attempts of cities and towns to impose a tax on all who peddle, sell, or canvass. This was a usual license tax and not aimed particularly at religionists. In several cases, the Court vacillated as to whether such a tax could be collected on the sale of religious literature. Eventually the Court held that religious activities could not be taxed at all (*Follett* v. *McCormick,* 321 U.S. 573; 1944).

The most dramatic of all the issues raised by the Witnesses was that of the compulsory flag salute. Using the First Commandment as their authority, the Witnesses refused to salute the flag or let their children do so. As a result of tremendous resentment about this refusal, a large number of states passed laws making saluting the flag in school mandatory. A pupil who refused to salute would be expelled. In *Minersville School District* v. *Gobitis* (310 U.S. 586; 1940), the Court held that a West Virginia statute did not unconstitutionally restrict freedom of religion. Mr. Justice Frankfurter gave the opinion of the majority and there was only one dissent, by Mr. Justice Stone.

Gradually, members of the Court appeared to develop uneasy consciences over the Gobitis decision. In addition, membership on the Court changed. In any event, the Gobitis case was overruled by a five-to-four decision in *West Virginia State Board of Education* v. *Barnette* (319 U.S. 624; 1943). Mr. Justice Jackson, delivering the opinion of the Court, issued some prose of a high literary order. In what was one of the high-water marks of devotion to the First Amendment, the Justice said:

> If there is any fixed star in our constitutional constellation, it is that no official, high or petty, can prescribe what shall be orthodox in politics, nationalism, religion, or other matters of opinion or force citizens to confess by word or act their faith therein. If there are any circumstances which permit an exception, they do not now occur to us.

What is so remarkable about the decision in the Barnette case is that it was rendered during wartime, when civil liberties generally were under intense pressures. Under such circumstances the observations of Mr. Jackson took on a special significance.

Compilers of constitutional casebooks divide the First

Amendment's freedom of religion provisions into two sections. The first part reads: "Congress shall make no law respecting an establishment of religion. . . ." We shall briefly consider this clause in connection with the situation present when two church groups contest with each other in order to obtain different types of government action.

For the type of situation at present under discussion, the second clause of the amendment is more relevant: ". . . or prohibiting the free exercise thereof." What did and did not constitute "free exercise" was extremely murky until the Witnesses fought it out with state and local authorities. (Federal laws as such were not at stake.) By their fanaticism and refusal to compromise with the state, this marginal and unorthodox religious group managed to spur the Supreme Court into defining (one could even say enlarging) the religious liberties of all Americans.[7]

Church Fighting Church over Government Programs

Speaking of education, the late President Kennedy declared in his second address on the State of the Union:

> I sent to Congress last year a proposal for federal aid to public school construction and teachers' salaries. I believe that bill, which passed the Senate and received House Committee approval, offered the minimum amount required by our needs and—in terms of across-the-board aid—the maximum scope permitted by our Constitution. I therefore see no reason to weaken or withdraw that bill; and I urge its passage at this session.[8]

The President neatly summarized the sorry results of a year's attempt by his Administration to secure passage of the first general aid to education bill. It is not the purpose in this commentary to trace in any detail the legislative history of the President's request or the specific reasons for its failure. Our concern rather is with the general reaction of the churches as they tried from various angles to affect the proposed legislation.

During the 1960 Presidential campaign, one of Mr. Kennedy's task forces had made a report recommending financial assistance to all public schools. Francis Cardinal Spellman, Roman Catholic Archbishop of New York, joined the fray in January 1961 by publicly criticizing this recommendation on the ground it "would discriminate against a multitude of children because their parents choose to exercise their constitutional right to educate them in accordance with their religious belief."[9]

The President himself, relying on the Supreme Court decisions relating to the establishment of religion clause of the First Amendment, said on March 1, in answer to a question asked at a press conference, that federal aid to a parochial school would be unconstitutional. He cited the case of *Everson* v. *Board of Education* (330 U.S. 1; 1947). In this case the Court by a five-to-four decision permitted a local community to provide bus rides to non-public-school children. This was the case in which Mr. Justice Black, speaking for the Court, gave his famous definition of what the establishment of religion clause means. He said, in part: "No tax in any amount, large or small, can be levied to support any religious activities or institutions, whatever they may be called, or whatever form they may adopt to teach or practice religion."

In view of the formulation of the Roman Catholic position, pressure rose on the General Board of the National Council of Churches to affirm a distinctly Protestant position. On an emergency basis, a text was prepared for consideration by the General Board of the National Council, meeting at Syracuse, New York, late in February 1961. Though the text itself was drafted very quickly, it should be noted that two divisions of the National Council had been at work on the problems involved in any federal aid bill for at least two years. Consequently, the words were well chosen and carried conviction. This is shown by the vote of the General Board: 87 for, 1 against, and no abstentions.

The pronouncement said, among other things: "We reaffirm our support of the public school system as an indispensable means of providing educational opportunity for all children; we urge provision of increased resources for the operation and improvement of the public schools; we declare our wholehearted support of the principle of public control of public funds."[10] Part 2 of the follow-up declaration asserted: "We oppose grants from federal, state, or local tax funds for nonpublic elementary and secondary schools."[11]

On March 2, the National Catholic Welfare Conference, which had been meeting in Washington, came out strongly for aid to parochial schools. Paragraph (4) of its declaration said: "In the event that a federal aid program is enacted which excludes children in private schools, these children will be the victims of discriminatory legislation. There will be no alternative but to oppose such discrimination."[12]

The Catholic statement also brought in a new dimension to the President's proposal when it called for an amendment to include "long-term, low-interest loans to private institutions."

The National Council pronouncement had made no reference to the possibility of loans. Consequently, when the spokesman for the Council appeared before the appropriate House and Senate subcommittees to present the Council's pronouncement, he had to express a private judgment with respect to loans. On this question he said, in essence, that he felt that an overwhelming majority of his General Board would have opposed loans if the question had come up. This view was subsequently upheld when the General Board, meeting in Chicago in June 1963, passed a resolution opposing loans for classroom construction. The loan provision had been added as a proposed extension of the National Defense Education Act, and had been approved by Catholic spokesmen as acceptable to them.

Protestant reaction was interesting, especially from the perspective of the student of contemporary affairs. The Baptist Joint Committee on Public Affairs, the leaders of the National Lutheran Council, spokesmen for the National Association of Evangelicals, and the United Christian Missionary Society (Disciples of Christ) all jumped on the band-wagon to denounce federal aid for private schools. The Lutheran Church-Missouri Synod and the Seventh-day Adventist

Church, both of which operate private schools, declared that they did not want federal funds. Subsequently, the United Presbyterians, meeting in General Assembly in Buffalo, took the position that there should be no federal aid for private schools.

As a result of these declarations, the National Council was applauded for taking the lead among Protestants in demanding that no federal aid go to church-supported elementary and secondary schools. On the other hand, it is curious that no large Protestant denomination through its governing assembly supported the position of the National Council that the Congress should enact into law the President's basic proposals, that is, federal aid for classroom construction of public schools and for salaries of public-school teachers. Protestant groups were apparently willing for the National Council to take the leadership in opposing the National Catholic Welfare Conference. When it came to accepting the Council's call to rally behind the President, Protestant groups became unreceptive or even hostile.

How the question may ultimately be settled is not our concern at this point. What has been illustrated is a situation where two powerful religious agencies, the National Catholic Welfare Conference and the National Council of Churches, fought each other in an effort to influence Congressional action on an issue that seemed to each side to be of basic significance. Each agency tried to present an argument based on the constitutional positions developed by its own lawyers, as had the Administration, the third party to the debate. Yet basically the debate, while it had constitutional aspects, became more and more a question of varying definitions of what is or is not in the public interest.

Other groups, of course, were involved in this struggle—to mention but a few, the teachers' organizations, the labor unions, the United States Chamber of Commerce, and the National Association of Manufacturers. The first two were for and the second two were against the President's proposals, as anyone would have expected. Makeshift as well as permanent state and local interest groups exerted pressures on Congressmen. It became a battle royal. This having been said, the most heat thus far has been generated by the church-state issue. And this particular illustration of that issue shows every sign of remaining of great importance in American politics. Should, for instance, demands for federal aid to private schools be turned down, this would probably in the first instance merely mean that the battlefield had been for the moment transferred from Congress to state legislatures.

No one should suppose that the positions taken by spokesmen for the leading religious groups are necessarily unchangeable. On the whole question of federal aid, the present Catholic position represents a sharp reversal of the attitude previously taken by leading Catholic spokesmen. So far as the Protestants are concerned, detached observers have questioned the consistency of their position. How can Protestant colleges accept federal money, while Protestant leaders, at the same time, denounce federal aid for church-related elementary and secondary schools? In addition, it is asked, how can Protestant hospitals and other welfare enterprises accept federal money in the light of the attitudes often expressed by Protestant leaders? There are other inconsistencies in both Catholic and Protestant positions that are far from resolved.

This discussion of the school question brings to a close the analysis of accommodation and conflict in current church-state relations. Returning to the conceptual framework of group theory with which the chapter began, we can see that the over-all typology and the specific illustrations support certain generalizations about the relationships of the government and the churches. There is always evident some degree of tension in the relationships. Despite such tension, government and the churches are much more often in agreement than in disagreement. Agreement is possible most of the time because the claims of church and state upon the citizens overlap—which is to say potentially conflict—only in the area of social control. Even here, accommodation rather than disagreement is the usual solution, and equilibrium is accordingly reached. Open conflict between church and state is a rarity, and can only happen where one or the other side violently transcends the traditional boundaries as defined by federal and state constitutions and as supported by custom and consensus.

CHAPTER FIVE

The Churches as Interest Groups

Many an otherwise staid citizen has turned apoplectic over his breakfast newspaper when confronted by such headlines as "Bishop Denounces Education Commissioner" or "Church Council Deplores Police Laxity" or "Rabbi Condemns Bingo." In a rage, he has turned to his wife and shouted: "Why don't the clergy stick to religion? Why do they have to meddle in politics?"

Such reactions, which may range from violent criticism to indulgent amusement, ought to be distinguished from simple anticlericalism, for there may be many grounds for taking exception to public utterances by clergymen prominent enough to obtain newspaper coverage. One very common ground is the belief that a large percentage of public statements issued by clergymen are negative: someone is usually "deploring" or "abhorring" or "condemning." Another objection stems from doubt that the persons quoted by the newspapers are actually the experts that their statements imply. This belief is especially current when deans of cathedrals and archbishops pose as critics of the cinema one day and specialists on United Nations affairs the next. Such universally claimed expertise goes contrary to the experience of most citizens, who live in a world peopled largely by specialists.

More serious, of course, is the implied criticism that the churches—for which the clergymen in question are presumably speaking—have exceeded the bounds of their legitimate concerns when they comment on nonparish problems. At this point an important issue is raised, which must be noted even though it cannot be settled here: Should the churches stick to "religion," defined in the narrow sense of personal devotion and piety, or should they feel obliged to apply their moral principles to all aspects of life? In principle—no matter how often they actually practice it—most of the leading religious bodies subscribe to the broader interpretation. In practice, severe limitations may exist, especially at the parish or local-church level. Further, some church bodies that are perfectly willing to speak out on what they consider social issues —alcohol, for instance—may be quite unwilling to take positions on what they deem political issues—such as the treaty limiting nuclear explosions. The very knowledge that many laymen make this distinction undoubtedly has influenced ecclesiastical officials.

Yet despite misgivings or even avowed hostility by some laymen and clergymen, most of the great churches of the nation do support and encourage diverse forms of political action. Such action may range from merely suggesting that constituents write to government officials to actually dispatching paid representatives to appear before legislators and administrators. The action, whatever it is, may imply almost no sanctions or a great many of them. It does not much matter whether the call to action comes from a board or committee, on the one hand, or an individual such as a bishop, on the other, provided that the source be legitimate.

Questions of legitimacy and of sanctions aside, the key consideration is whether a group tries through political means to make its own views those of the general public. If it does, it is an interest group, and in this sense the Protestant Episcopal Church, the National Lutheran Council, and the Association of Churches of Greater Houston are all interest groups. Some church groups are obviously more active in politics than others, and the type of organization for political follow-up varies widely. In some cases, the responsibility for implementing the decisions of the policy-makers will rest in the hands of editors of church publications; in other cases, a local clergyman may be designated to take the necessary action. The largest groups, such as the Roman Catholic Church and the National Council of Churches, maintain offices staffed with specialists on national legislative matters. The same principle of specialization is followed in some Catholic dioceses and in some state and local councils of churches.

An interest group may or may not engage in lobbying, as that term is defined in federal and state statutes. Universally, church groups argue that they are exempt from the laws because—as Luke Ebersole wryly noted in his study *Church Lobbying in the Nation's Capitol*—they claim to be basically "educational" in nature.[1] For the most part, legislators have either taken the churches' assertion at face value or have construed the laws broadly. This is not merely a conspiracy to aid religion, for the churches do all within their power to stress that their main concern is to educate their own members, for example, through periodicals published by their Washington offices. In recent years, the churches have tended to abandon the once popular "social education and action" in favor of such expressions as "the church and society" or "life and work"—in an obvious effort to play down the activist emphasis of the earlier formula. In addition, only small amounts of the time and money of the principal social action units are devoted directly toward influencing pending legislative and administrative decisions. In this manner, the religious agencies escape the registration requirements of the lobbying laws while retaining their freedom to lobby.[2] From their point of view, it is an ideal arrangement, though it is doubtful that the supposed subterfuge deceives anyone. It is simply not very good politics to question the good faith of the churches!

THE EFFECTIVENESS OF INTEREST GROUPS

The effectiveness of interest groups is conditioned by a whole series of factors, which may be divided for the sake of convenience into internal, external, and inter-group elements. Considered from this point of view, the churches are as typical or atypical as farmers organizations, labor unions, business groups—in short, the other great interests into which American life is sectioned. The churches differ from each other in their attitudes toward political action and in their organization for it. Yet these differences are of degree, not of kind, and the same analytical methods that have proved of value in examining labor unions or veterans organizations are also useful in assessing the churches.

The relationship between the leaders and the led, which may be quite simple at the local church level, may become exceedingly complex at the highest judicatories. In some churches the highest figures are chosen from the top, not elected by assemblies. The Roman Catholic Church, where the bishops are appointed by the Pope, is the best illustration. When an individual bishop speaks out on a political matter (even if it is termed by him a "moral" matter), he does not in theory have to worry about his relationship with his followers. Yet it is almost inconceivable in the United States that an ecclesiastical official, no matter what the form of government of his church, would not at least take into account the probable reactions of his own constituents. He would not be bound by those reactions, but he surely would not brush them aside. At the other extreme is the minister whose denomination in effect has no hierarchy; the result is that theoretically he can only do what his congregation specifically dictates. Again, in practice, local church boards in the United States normally allow some leeway to ministers who have no hierarchy to protect them. The bishop is not quite the free agent he seems to be, nor is the Baptist or Congregational minister necessarily in fact the prisoner of the local congregation.

The relationship of the clergy to the laymen affects, then, the ability of church groups to act in politics, and so does the relationship between the higher and the lower clergy. Even in those churches where in principle there is no "higher" clergy (where the doctrine is every minister a "bishop"), the fact remains that some ministers are more important, more powerful, and better paid than others. The situation is especially apparent in many of the old-line Protestant denominations, where the top administrative positions—national and regional—are held by careerists. It is risky for a young clergyman in these churches to support political stands that are disapproved by or are simply unpopular with his superiors.

These and other internal factors determine an interest group's cohesiveness, its ability to present a united front to the world, and its ability to claim a massive following. External factors are also of great significance, for a rhetorically brilliant statement of political position built on a large base of followers would not by itself result in political accomplishment. Churchmen must also work to achieve their political goals. (It is not just a difference between education and action—as the church slogans sometimes imply; for action is, in the best sense, education.)

In their organizing efforts to reach government officials churches show their greatest diversity. Some churches apparently believe that no particular organization is necessary and that a statement issued to the press in and of itself accomplishes worthwhile objectives. No further buttressing is therefore considered desirable. Other churches, in the manner of the great national economic interests, have established Washington offices and offices in state capitals to secure continuing representation before government and consultation by government. More and more this has become the accepted practice.

To influence the government directly may require a Washington office, or its state and local equivalent, but to influence the general public in order to influence the government indirectly requires a mass media apparatus. All principal American churches now have public information or news offices, the aim of which is to provide press, radio, and TV coverage of denominational activities. The two most effective of these agencies are undoubtedly those maintained by the National Catholic Welfare Conference and the National Council of Churches. In addition, the leading church bodies have broadcasting units, either as part of an over-all information organization or as separate agencies. The chief purpose of such units is to provide a channel for placing religious fare on the airwaves, but some programs may also have a public-interpretation function. A splendid example of this latter approach was the production and placement on TV stations by the National Catholic Welfare Conference of short motion pictures designed to explain the Catholic position on the Kennedy Administration's aid-to-education bills. In clarity of story-line and photography the pictures equaled the very best commercially produced programs.

Another principal factor affecting an interest group's impact on government is the caliber of its representatives, both those who may appear intermittently to testify and those who are responsible for following legislative developments. Fortunately, the churches can, and do, produce highly regarded witnesses, especially on significant questions such as overseas relief. These witnesses may be church officials or they may be laymen of special distinction in their fields. Persons who are on the payrolls of the churches and who hold the responsibility for continuing liaison with legislative matters vary widely in terms of background and ability, as would be expected. A great deal depends on the tradition of the particular religious group—whether it has historically been on speaking terms with government or in opposition to government. For whatever specific reasons—and there may be many—the Quakers, organized as the American Friends Service Committee, and the Brethren and the Mennonites have been second to no other groups in their ability to gain government support and sympathy for relief programs. Their representatives long ago proved their expertise in this area.

There is, finally, a third set of factors that helps determine how effective a religious interest group will be. This last element consists of the relationships among the different groups and raises the question of how well they work together or in opposition. For highly divided groups—especially the Protestants, but also the Jews—a cardinal question is whether there is sufficient consensus to establish a united front. It is evident that a high degree of cohesiveness inside various Protestant churches will not mean much politically if they adopt mutually contradictory stands. It is equally apparent that if those churches go one way—against federal aid to public schools, for instance—and their National Council's General Board goes the other way—by endorsing such aid—the end result is only confusion. (They are in agreement only in opposing federal aid to private, meaning mostly parochial, schools!)

Church bodies rarely work in isolation in political matters, and their working with nonreligious groups offers almost limitless possibilities. The brunt of the battle for federal aid to education was borne by the National Education Association and related groups, not by Protestant churches. Efforts to change the immigration laws have been spearheaded by ethnic organizations, with assists from the churches, especially the Catholic Church. Jewish secular organizations have usually taken the leadership in civil-rights matters, and the Jewish religious organizations have lent their support.

The American Jewish Committee, the American Jewish Congress, and the Anti-Defamation League of B'nai B'rith have been especially active in the campaigns to protect civil liberties and to expand civil rights. Concerning the purposes of the three groups, the *American Jewish Year Book* reports as follows: American Jewish Committee (founded 1906)—"Seeks to prevent infraction of the civil and religious rights of Jews in any part of the world and to secure equality of economic, social, and educational opportunity through education and civic action . . ."; American Jewish Congress (founded 1917)—"Seeks to eliminate all forms of racial and religious bigotry; to advance civil rights, protect civil liberties, and defend religious freedom and separation of church and state . . ."; Anti-Defamation League of B'nai B'rith (founded 1913)—"Seeks to eliminate defamation of Jews, counteract un-American and antidemocratic propaganda, and promote better group relations."[3]

In contrast to these organizations, which are considered political and secular, is the Synagogue Council of America. The Synagogue Council "acts as the over-all Jewish religious representative body of Orthodox, Conservative, and Reform Judaism in the United States vis-à-vis the Catholic and Protestant national agencies, the U.S. government, and the United Nations."[4] The Council represented Judaism in the tri-faith representations that were made before Congressional committees during 1963 on behalf of strong civil-rights legislation. On a different level of activity, the Council took the leadership in protesting to the Soviet government certain anti-Semitic practices that it charged had occurred in the Soviet Union in the early 1960's. In order to achieve the maximum results the Council quietly sought and obtained cooperation in this endeavor from groups representing the other two great faiths in the United States.

These illustrations are not meant to belittle the efforts of churches as interest groups; they are meant rather to underscore the idea that religious bodies are normally only part of a very much wider alliance. Part of the task of the political practitioner—whether a member of the legislature or of a private group—is to pull together the diverse elements favoring a bill or program in order to build up maximum support. To be successful, such an effort requires the very highest kind of ability in bargaining and in negotiating, and this talent is in short supply. It is commonly believed that former Senators and Congressmen, because of their understanding of the complexities of the legislative process, make superior strategists. If so, it is worth noting that while quite a few former legislators represent business, labor, and other powerful interests as Washington representatives, few if any have ever represented the churches and synagogues.

ORGANIZATION AND ROLES

Catholics

The national coordinating agency for the Roman Catholic Church—the National Catholic Welfare Conference—is located in Washington, as are various agencies of Protestant churches and councils. This simple geographical fact has led to the deepest confusions, distrust, and cynicism concerning the motives of the churches. Many Protestant laymen, especially those whose zeal to preserve the status quo paradoxically leads them to adopt an unwitting but quasi-Marxist view of human motivation, have convinced themselves that the denominational Washington offices are trying to take over the government, preferably by underhanded methods. The following observations are intended to clear up these confusions.

The predecessor to the present National Catholic Welfare Conference was formed in 1917 in fulfillment of a pledge made by Cardinal Gibbons to President Wilson that Catholics would do their share in winning the war.[5] The original objective was therefore to provide for the religious and recreational welfare of Catholics serving in the armed forces. So successful was the temporary organization that the American bishops established the agency on a permanent basis in 1919. There was some initial confusion because the term "council" in the original title seemed to imply legislative powers. Consequently, this term was changed to "conference," and beginning in 1923 the NCWC became the National Catholic Welfare Conference.

The NCWC is therefore the instrument of the American bishops. At the same time, the autonomy of each diocese is guaranteed. The organization is voluntary, in that it depends for membership and support on the free choice of each bishop, and it has no compulsory authority. A bishop may align himself with it or not.

Except to specialists, the general organizational structure of the NCWC is of no particular interest. The two departments of greatest relevance to political matters are the Social Action Department and the Legal Department. In an official brochure, the social action group makes clear what it is and is not: it is not an organization "formed to act" and it has "no legislative powers." "It is a clearing house for the distribution of the best Catholic study in the social action field and, thus, is primarily educational in its purpose."[6]

The Social Action Department has as its goal "a society permeated with the ideals of justice and charity, directed toward the aim of restoring all things in Christ."[7] To this end, it interests itself in such fields as industrial relations, interracial relations, social work, family life, and international relations. The Department tries to achieve its goal through conferences and publications, and there has been extensive cooperation over the years with corresponding Protestant and Jewish religious groups. For example, as far back as 1923, the Department, in conjunction with other religious groups, sponsored a joint statement condemning the twelve-hour working day.

It is the work of the Legal Department of the NCWC that causes Protestant envy and perhaps some occasional Catholic misgivings, for it is this agency's primary obligation "to keep abreast of all legislative and judicial developments that affect the interests of the Church, either favorably or adversely, especially matters that are national in scope and which involve a religious or moral issue." The major categories of concern are therefore federal legislation, government regulations, and court decisions. The Department analyzes proposed and enacted legislation, evaluates legislation and makes action recommendations to other units of the NCWC, assists in preparing statements to be made before Congressional committees, represents the NCWC before administrative agencies, and surveys court decisions. In addition, the Legal Department has other duties—for example, cooperating with diocesan attorneys. The executive staff of the Department consists of five full-time lawyers, a small number considering the extraordinarily heavy and complex assignments involved.

Ordinarily testimony given before Congressional committees or government regulatory agencies is delivered by the head of the NCWC department whose work is most clearly related to the matter under consideration. In the various hearings held on the Kennedy Administration's proposals for federal aid to education, Monsignor Frederick G. Hochwalt usually presented the views of the NCWC. The staff of the Legal Department stayed in the background, although it was responsible for the massive legal briefs relied on by the Education Department. The bulk of contacts between the Legal Department and agencies of the federal government is, as might be imagined, informal, and the liaison is two-way. It is common practice for a government official to request the assistance of the NCWC, usually through its Legal Department, for help in the formulation of regulations.

Jews

Jewish interests vis-à-vis the federal government are represented through the Religious Action Center of the Union of American Hebrew Congregations, which has its own building on Washington's Massachusetts Avenue. Established by the Reformed wing of Judaism, the Center serves the needs of Orthodox and Conservative constituencies as well as those of the Reformed group. It does so by acting as the Washington agency of the Synagogue Council of America, which is the over-all representative body of Orthodox, Conservative, and Reformed Judaism in the United States. The purpose of the Center is to carry out "the religious dimension of social action," and to this end a staff of about fifteen persons is employed. During the latter half of 1963, the Center's staff played an active role in the effort to secure passage of the strongest possible civil-rights measures.

Protestants

Protestant agencies in Washington—those of cooperative bodies as well as of individual denominations—follow the same general organization and representation as their Jewish and Catholic counterparts. But there are significant differences in actual operation, differences that on balance considerably weaken Protestant efforts. The most obvious is that Catholic influence flows normally through one channel—the NCWC—while Protestant influences very often meander through a series of passages.

In an effort to arrive at greater Protestant consensus, the National Council of Churches—the cooperative agency of some 31 Protestant and Orthodox denominations—established a Washington Office. It was the goal of this unit to perform for Protestantism and Orthodoxy the type of service rendered for Catholicism by various units of the NCWC, notably the Legal Department. The staff of the Washington Office was headed by an assistant general secretary, who was directly responsible to the general secretary (or his deputy) at NCC headquarters in New York City. In a further effort to strengthen its Washington outpost, the National Council set up an advisory committee of District of Columbia clergymen and government officials. Since the committee had no policy functions, it is apparent that its chief raison d'être was to facilitate contacts between the NCC and government.

The Washington Office of the NCC was charged with following legislation and reporting pertinent developments back to the principal NCC operating divisions in New York City, arranging for officers or staff of the NCC to appear before Congressional committees and government agencies, making representations to government as necessary, and helping government agencies to obtain information or reactions to proposals.

So far, the Legal Department of the NCWC and the Washington Office of the NCC appear to be similar organizations, and in concept they are. Yet the Protestant agency is far less effective than its Catholic counterpart, and for at least three very understandable reasons. The first reason has already been touched on—the fact that the Washington Office of the NCC is only one of scores of Protestant "offices" in the nation's capital, which means that the problem of coordination is always difficult and sometimes impossible.

Most of the largest Protestant denominations that are members of the NCC have offices of some sort in Washington. These range from almost hidden observation posts intended to scan the current Congressional conflict (as with the United Presbyterian Church's lone observer) to full-fledged major agencies of a denomination (as with the Methodist Church's General Board of Christian Social Concerns). In addition—and it is a most significant addition—denominations which are not members of the NCC (such as the Seventh-day Adventists), nondenominational quasi-religious groups (such as Protestants and Other Americans United for the Separation of Church and State), and confessional alliances (such as the

Baptist World Alliance) have headquarters in Washington.

It is easy to sympathize with the young lawyer for a government regulatory agency who spent his first day on the job trying to find out for his superior "Protestant reaction" to the draft of a proposed regulation. "Sir," he is said to have reported grimly, "I can find lots of Protestants in this city, but I'm afraid I can't give you *a* Protestant reaction." The official was not in the least perturbed. "All right," he said, "in that case call up my pastor. We'll simply assume his reaction is typical."

The multiplicity of Protestant representation is the most important single factor limiting the effectiveness of the Washington Office of the National Council of Churches. (There is nothing the Council as such can do about this, for its constitution prohibits it from participating in efforts to merge constituent denominations.)

Another factor is simply the smallness of the staff, especially of specialists in governmental affairs. At the end of the 1960–63 triennium of the National Council, its Washington Office had only three full-time executives, of whom one was a political scientist, one a lawyer, and one a clergyman. Now it is true that the denominations can and do on occasion lend social action specialists to the Washington Office—put them on detached service, as it were—but the result is a far cry from the careful and continuing work of the NCWC's Legal Department. In any event, these specialists are subject-matter experts, for example, on international relations; they are never lawyers, but usually ministers, and they ordinarily carry denominational as well as NCC portfolios simultaneously. They are therefore not in a position to give the kind of detailed and expert counsel in legislative and administrative matters which the NCWC is accustomed to having.

A third factor affecting the National Council's Washington Office is the difficulty of obtaining adequate public support for a position that has been publicly taken. It is a problem which is endemic in Protestantism, but it is particularly apparent from the perspective of Washington. Two reactions during the discussions on the Kennedy Administration's proposals to aid public schools illustrate the difficulty. The nation's press gave excellent coverage to the NCC pronouncement calling for support of the President's program. Subsequently, reporting of NCC testimony before Congressional committees was also extensive. There was no favoritism, for the Catholic positions were likewise reported in detail. However, as the debates warmed up and as the protagonists cast charity to the winds, a strange phenomenon developed: thousands of Catholic pupils in parochial schools filled out postcards "demanding" aid for Catholic schools, and they sent these cards to the Congressmen from their districts. In one respect, the performance was amusing, and could be attributed to the overzealousness of the nun-teachers. In another respect, the avalanche of cards was anything but humorous to the Congressmen, who were aware of the fact that the students had parents who could vote.

To come quickly to the point, the expected Protestant flood of letters in support of the NCC's stand never materialized. Despite vigorous NCC efforts to prod the constituent denominations to have their laymen write letters, few letters ever arrived in Washington. The failure is even more astounding when it is realized that the NCC pronouncement was initially drafted by representatives of the very denominational educational units that had the responsibility inside their denominations to follow up any educational resolutions adopted by the National Council. It could not, in short, have been honestly contended that the responsible denominational agencies had been taken unawares by the Council's vote. What is illustrated by this case—and others of equal pertinence could be cited—is how the lack of follow-up machinery to demonstrate popular support seriously weakens presentations arranged for by the NCC's Washington Office. No matter how brilliant the wording of a statement nor how effective its exposition, the naked fact remains that it must command reasonable support "back home"—or it is a waste of everybody's time. There must, further, be some way of demonstrating this support, for instance, through letters or telegrams or editorials or perhaps even parades in the streets.

THE PUBLIC IMAGE OF THE CLERGY

Walter Lippmann pointed out in *Public Opinion* that most of us tend to think in terms of what he called "stereotypes."[8] The name of a country is drawn to our attention and we promptly picture the land and its people not necessarily as they really are but as they have been caricatured to us. We do not do this deliberately; we simply do not have at our disposal the facts of the matter, or we are sufficiently prejudiced through having ingested incorrect information that we would not change our minds even in the presence of the facts.

Stereotypes—or public images, as we would say today—change but slowly. During a good part of our national history the stock comedy character was an Irishman. Subsequently, he left the stage to be replaced by representatives of other national groups. The image of the American Indian has enjoyed successive bear and bull markets, as has the image of the Swede, the Dutchman, and even the Turk—though few Americans until recent times had ever met a Turk. National characteristics, real or supposed, have always been fair game for humorists, and remain so.

It may not matter, except to a real Turk, what the American image or images may be of a Turk. But it makes a great deal of difference to leaders of significant American interest groups—business, labor, agriculture, veterans, or religious—how they are perceived by the general public. It makes a difference because the image affects the degree of seriousness that will be accorded what the leaders say and do. Religious leaders, like other public-opinion makers, are forced to take into account the public attitudes toward them as persons.

This consideration is much more than a mere concern over personal status, for it is based on the conviction that the public in some measure judges an organization by the people who lead it. For the good of the organization, then, it is advisable, perhaps imperative, that the public image of its leaders be such as to evoke a sympathetic reaction to what those leaders say and do. In the case of the churches, the leaders are, of course, the clergy, a term which means a professional grouping. Inside the profession the gradations in respect to authority and status and income are often marked. Yet for purposes of general analysis it is logical to consider the clergy as a group in much the same way as one considers physicians a distinctive profession. In this way it is possible to arrive at certain general statements as to public attitudes toward the professional group as a whole.

Present-day social scientists trying to determine what the public (or publics) thinks of a particular group can bring into play a whole battery of scientific devices that will result in precise, quantitative answers. Unfortunately, this procedure is only a generation or so old, so that it is necessary to use a different approach in order to arrive at attitude changes over a longer time. A convenient method is to examine popular views toward a professional group, in this case the clergy, as shown in the literature of particular periods.

Horton Davies in *A Mirror of the Ministry in Modern Novels* has made this sort of examination, and some of what he has to report is directly pertinent to the problem of how novelists have regarded the clergy as the living symbols of ecclesiastical authority.[9] A general conclusion is that "Catholic priests seem to have been more successfully delineated than Protestant ministers."[10] For this two reasons are ventured, of which the first is the more familiar. It is simply that the Catholic priest in fiction offers greater dramatic possibilities, for instance, through immediate identification because of his distinctive dress. But there is a more basic reason: the priest is held to possess "a magisterial authority" in contrast to the minister who has only "ministerial authority."

Another advantage held by the priests—in the view of the novelists studied by Davies—lies in the refusal to identify Catholicism with the "American way of life." Opposed to this is the tendency of the novelists to show Protestantism not so much as a religion as a "moralism of respectability." Yet in the case of both priests and ministers the clergyman who is successfully portrayed "counts the world well lost"—he is *contra mundum.*

The reverse is also true, for clergymen who fall prey to the blandishments of this world are considered by the writers to be failures. This is the theme, of course, of Sinclair Lewis's controversial book *Elmer Gantry*. A more recent illustration of the same motif comes from Eve McFall's play, *The Case Against Eve*.[11] The story is ostensibly about the trial of a suburban housewife, but the basic point is to show how a woman manages to estrange herself from God. It is not altogether her fault, for the principal characters in her life, including the local minister, help push her into a meaningless existence. The function of the minister is to sanctify the status quo, a physical as well as psychological condition from which the leading character of the play needs desperately to escape.

An altogether different method of analyzing the place of clergymen in fiction is employed by Willard Thorp in an essay entitled "The Religious Novel as Best Seller in America."[12] Thorp examines the best-selling novels in various periods of American life and speculates as to why they did so well. He defines a religious novel as one "whose *main* concern is to present a sermon in the guise of a story (mere piety is not enough)."[13] A "best seller" is considered a book the circulation of which was believed to have equaled 1 per cent of the population of the United States for the decade in which it was published.[14]

On this basis, the first religious novel to become a best seller was written by the Rev. William Ware and published in 1837. It was entitled *Letters of Lucius M. Piso, from Palmyra to his Friend Marcus Curtius at Rome*. This and many other novels of the early nineteenth century emphasized the plight of Christians in the Roman world. During this period contemporary American clergymen as the subjects of novels received very little if any attention. The fascination with problems of early Christianity reached a peak with the publication in 1880 of General Lew Wallace's *Ben-Hur, A Tale of the Christ*, the most popular religious novel ever written in America.

A second phase in the development of the religious novel found writers concentrating on practical piety and on conversions to Christianity. Among the most successful writers of this period was the Rev. E. P. Roe. By the time he had published his fourth book—*Opening a Chestnut Burr* (1874)—Roe had convinced himself that he should leave the ministry in order to reach a larger audience by writing his "sermons in the form of fiction."[15] In the work of Roe and others of his conviction the type of Christianity that emerges is highly individualistic. The concept of a corporate ministry is missing.

In the latter half of the nineteenth century, some Americans were troubled by the seeming inconsistencies between the new precepts of science and orthodox Christian beliefs. More particularly, the Darwinian theory of evolution appeared to undercut the account of creation recorded in Genesis. Novelists eagerly seized upon this theme but very few of the science-versus-religion books became best sellers.

In contrast, the Social Gospel movement—a powerful drive for social reform led by prominent Protestant ministers—stimulated novelists to write several books that became exceptionally popular. In the novels portraying the Social Gospel movement the young, dedicated clergyman is the hero, and he is very much of an activist. It often happened in this period, as it had in an earlier period, that the author of a best-selling work about a clergyman was himself a minister. At the beginning of the Social Gospel period the Rev. Charles M. Sheldon was prominent as a writer of religious novels, as was the late Rev. Harold Bell Wright (1872–1944), whose life spanned the Social Gospel cycle. Wright centered his attention upon the ills of society, which, like many another Protestant minister, he found disproportionately concentrated in urban areas!

Thorp believes that the religious novel is as popular in this country today as it ever was. But the emphasis has shifted from belief to actual behavior. Reliance on Scriptural authority has declined, and its place has been taken by a concern for making ethical decisions. As a result, writers try to demonstrate that Christianity will lead to a more abundant life or to a greater sense of self-confidence. Thorp cites the Rev. Lloyd C. Douglas (1877–1951) as a good illustration of authors who write in this genre. In *Green Light* (1935) the leading character—Dean Harcourt of Trinity Cathedral—is pictured as an "inexhaustible fount of spiritual power." No problem defies his healing solution. The universe is on his side; he "gets" the "Green Light."

In the books of Douglas and others like him the concept of authority is a highly personal one, for authority runs through a direct pipeline from God to the clergyman-hero. Little or no acceptance of the idea that the church itself is a source of authority is implicit, and there is none of the social purpose and collective militancy that characterized the Social Gospel movement. The presumption is that the church speaks to individuals through gifted ministers who head local congregations. If this is the case, it follows that public statements and appeals by high denominational leaders and top governing assemblies are at best unnecessary and at worst likely to be erroneous. Whether he meant to or not, Douglas as a novelist accurately reflected one of the main currents in contemporary Protestantism when he stressed its localism. (Of course, this has also been one of the principal *problems* of Protestantism, but this aspect of the question did not concern Douglas.)

Only in recent times have books with a Roman Catholic religious theme made the best-seller lists. Russell Janney's *The Miracle of the Bells* (1946) and Henry Morton Robinson's *The Cardinal* (1950) both enjoyed tremendous success. The latter is pure Horatio Alger fiction and received a chilly reception from the Catholic intelligentsia. A very different type of book is Edwin O'Connor's *Edge of Sadness,* which is the story of a priest who wins his battle against alcoholism and eventually settles down in a deteriorating inner-city parish. The book is intensely personal in tone and does not at all involve social action.

Novels that stress Jewish *religious* themes are scarce and do not seem to have made any best-seller lists. There are, on the other hand, a great many novels and short stories that explore Jewish *family* life. It would be useful to have a study of American rabbis as viewed by novelists, playwrights, and poets, and perhaps such an examination will be forthcoming. Also of value would be an analysis of Eastern Orthodox priests, a group which is just beginning to receive general recognition in the United States.

Folklore, songs, and popular jokes reveal a good deal about public attitudes toward institutions and their leaders. Under conditions of a police state, with its attendant control of the mass media, the only method of gauging popular feelings may be to rely on the songs and stories of ordinary people. Yet even in a society where the mass media are not censored by government, there may exist a significant *attitudinal* difference between what is said in polite society and what is uttered when the forces of respectability are not present. To be fair, any such testing should be tried across the board so that it includes, in addition to the clergy, some references to politicians, government officials, labor leaders, businessmen, and members of various professional groups.

Handled in this way, a careful analysis of popular attitudes toward clergymen would add a new dimension to the understanding of the place of religion in American life. A good place to start would be with missionaries, for there is a general impression that as a group they have fallen in popular esteem. During the great nineteenth-century expansion of Christianity, especially of Protestant Christianity, missionaries were considered heroes. They were felt to be persons worthy of general emulation.

Yet the popular status of a missionary has been downgraded in the last three or four decades. There have always been jokes about missionaries and cannibals, generally to the advantage of the cannibals. But it remained for the cultural anthropologists—who arrived on the same alien shores decades after the missionaries had landed—to furnish allegedly scientific reasons for ridiculing the churchmen. In particular, the "missionary position" in sexual intercourse and the imposition of "Mother Hubbards" in climates where they were inappropriate lent themselves to easy lampooning.

The state of war unilaterally declared by cultural anthropologists on overseas missionaries would not of itself account for the deromanticization of missionaries that has been evident in popular folklore since the early part of this century. There are undoubtedly more substantial reasons, such as the rise of nationalism in countries receiving large numbers of missionaries and the great increases in military and civilian foreign travel since our entry into the First World War in 1917. Yet the fact remains that furloughed missionaries, while they may still attract church audiences, are no longer the civic heroes they were fifty or more years ago. The civic spotlight has shifted toward the returned soldier or diplomat or even businessman.

THE CHURCHES' PERFORMANCE

A favorite American pastime is to rate organizations in terms of supposed effectiveness, as though they were football teams playing in the same league. An extreme example was a comparison of the Roman Catholic Church and the Standard Oil Company of New Jersey. In this case, it was found by the efficiency experts that the managements of the two institutions were roughly equal in proficiency. The presumption is that this information gladdened the hearts of stockholders and parishioners alike.

Despite the difficulties in trying to determine which religious group has the most effective "lobby," it is possible to cite particular successes. Unquestionably, the most successful religiously affiliated lobby ever to operate in Washington was that of the Anti-Saloon League which, under the leadership of the superb strategist Wayne B. Wheeler, deserves the lion's share of credit for the passage by Congress of the Prohibition Amendment.[16] Subsequently the League helped push the proposal through state conventions. The League was the creation of American Protestantism, which supported it through a score of ways. It was nonpartisan, nondenominational, single-purpose, fanatic, well organized, well financed, and brilliantly led. Its chief asset was its ability to capitalize on the latent predispositions of millions of Americans by transforming predispositions into positive political action.

Another feature of Anti-Saloon League activities is that the League concentrated on the *passage* of legislation. Ordinarily, religiously oriented and church groups concentrate their efforts on opposing the passage of pending bills, or in seeking repeal of statutes already in existence. A student of church political action—R. Morton Darrow—cites two such illustrations of church victories, both of which involve negative pressures.[17] The first was the successful effort by the National Catholic Welfare Conference, in 1938, to persuade various Congressmen to repudiate their signing of a petition in favor of pro-Loyalist Spain. The other was a Protestant endeavor, led by Presbyterians, which succeeded in keeping the universal military training bill bottled up in committee in 1948. However, related and repeated Protestant efforts to scrap selective service legislation were consistently defeated. The Protestant offensive to defeat President Truman's nomination of General Mark Clark as ambassador to the Vatican triumphed when General Clark withdrew his name from consideration by the Senate in January 1952.[18]

Spectacular, front-page controversies involving religious groups tend to obscure if not obliterate the occasions when functional units of national churches work quietly together in the pursuit of common legislative objectives. Such cooperation has been particularly noteworthy in the areas of the military chaplaincy, the resettlement of Cuban refugees, and support for certain United Nations activities. In these areas the theological differences among the leading churches are relatively subsumed under common agreement on objectives.

Despite occasional evidence of cooperation among the faiths at the middle and lower organizational levels, the general public impression of Protestant and Catholic relations has been that of frigidity, if not downright hostility. Nowhere has this impression received greater support than from the newspaper accounts of wranglings by religious leaders over legislative issues. It ordinarily seems safe to predict that if the National Catholic Welfare Conference favors a measure the National Council of Churches will try to rally the opposition. Or, at a local level, it appears that if a state council of churches takes one position the local Catholic prelates can be almost surely counted on to take an opposing one.

A dramatic change in the traditional attitudes was manifested during the summer of 1963 when top representatives of the National Council of Churches, the Roman Catholic

Church, and the Synagogue Council of America presented a joint statement to Congressional committees in support of the Kennedy Administration's proposed civil-rights legislation. Tri-faith cooperation also took place on a wide scale as representatives of leading religious groups joined to testify before state and local agencies of government in furtherance of Negro objectives. Going beyond mere testifying, numerous local religious groups worked together to assist Negro street demonstrations. In a sort of grand finale toward the end of the summer—on August 28—the National Council of Churches, the National Catholic Council for Interracial Justice, and the American Jewish Congress mobilized and dispatched thousands of individuals from across the country to participate in the gigantic "March on Washington." The Washington demonstration was initiated and managed by the principal Negro civil-rights organizations, and most of the demonstrators were Negroes. Yet the degree of cooperation among the three faiths as they pooled their resources to support the Negro demands was unprecedented in American history.

RESPONSIBILITY AND RESPONSIVENESS

The most crucial single factor in determining how much weight to attach to the testimony of any interest group is the integrity of the policy statement upon which the testimony is based. This consideration far transcends in importance the cleverness of the lobbyists or the skill of the publicists. In this sense "integrity" means far more than mere honesty, and it means more than just consistency. It involves elements of responsiveness and of responsibility, and is related—as are these two terms—to representativeness.

An example from a nonreligious source may be helpful in pursuing these distinctions. Several years ago the American Legion, at its annual national meeting, passed by vote of the overwhelming majority of the delegates a resolution denouncing UNESCO and demanding that the United States withdraw from it. On the face of it, such an action taken by the largest veterans organization might have been interpreted as a very significant rebuff of an important aspect of American foreign policy. Instead, the reaction of many mature newspapers was to write editorials which did not discuss the action voted but rather lectured the Legionnaires on democratic procedure.

It was possible for newspapers to write as they did because they were in possession of several pertinent facts, namely, that the delegates had not been notified prior to the convention that the issue would come up, that freedom of debate (on the testimony of the New York State representatives) had been curtailed during the convention, that a small group of policy-makers had railroaded the resolution through the great mass of uninterested delegates who were in Florida primarily to have a good time, not to discuss serious political issues. The editorials further drove home the point that the policy-makers, that is, the professional bureaucrats who ran the American Legion machinery in Indianapolis, were in no real sense responsible to the rank and file of Legionnaires and had neither the means nor the intention of consulting them. After what amounted to a national exposé of its procedures, the Legion could not seriously have supposed that its resolution on UNESCO could have been taken as necessarily representing anything but a small minority of its membership.

Two general questions may be put to all large groups that issue statements intended to affect public opinion or government action. The first involves the concept of responsibility: To what extent and through what means are the policy-makers responsible to the people whom they are supposed to represent? And the second involves the concept of responsiveness: To what extent and through what means may rank-and-file opinion be transmitted to those charged with the duty of issuing policy statements? The problem of responsibility varies with the particular church—its structure and its traditions. A message issued by the American Catholic bishops carries behind it the full weight of the Roman Catholic Church in America. Such a statement is official, and it is irrelevant that the bishops were chosen by the Pope and not elected and that the bishops did not first hold a referendum of forty million Catholics.

A resolution passed by a typical Protestant denomination, for example, the United Presbyterian Church meeting in General Assembly, is entirely different in kind and in effect. By the constitution of that church a social pronouncement is advisory on its constituents (the favorite newspaper expression is "not binding"). Its effect is held to be purely moral, but entitled to respect because it was arrived at by a responsible body after careful deliberation. This respect is derived not so much from the commissioners' credentials as from the percentage of the total religious body they actually represent. Thus it almost follows that if the Assembly were genuinely representative the pronouncement must have genuine merit.

Even more difficult to characterize is a pronouncement or other official statement issued by a council of sovereign denominations, such as the National Council of the Churches of Christ in the U.S.A. Both the Council's General Board (which holds interim authority and meets three times a year) and its General Assembly (which holds plenary power and meets once every three years) are intended to be as representative as possible of the denominations. It is in accordance with this principle that the denominations (which is to say their highest judicatories) elect representatives to the National Council. But the denominational top judicatories themselves may be only indirectly representative. For instance, in the United Presbyterian Church a layman is asked to vote once a year for church officers, and that is the extent of his balloting. The church officers in turn elect a layman to represent the congregation at the next governing level—called the presbytery—and the minister is automatically considered a member of the presbytery. It is the presbytery, in turn, which elects one or more ministers and one or more laymen (how many depends on the size of the presbytery, but clergy and laymen are chosen in equal numbers) to represent it at the annual denominational General Assembly. The distance from a local congregation to a General Assembly is therefore considerable, and from this perspective the National Council may appear to be well over the horizon!

Carried to an unchecked extreme the representative principle can result in pure anarchy, where nobody is really responsible to anyone but himself and therefore nothing can ever be done. The practical solution is to minimize representativeness and maximize responsibility. By concentrating authority in the hands of the professionals it is possible to move forward, and this is precisely what most Protestant denominations and their councils have done. In the absence of grass-roots polls or referenda, however, it becomes difficult to determine how widespread is the support for any particular pronouncement. The backing could be massive or, as in the case cited from the experience of the Legion, it theoretically could reflect only the views of the "insiders."

In actual fact, of course, the procedure followed by most Protestant denominations is quite unlike that observed by the Legion. It normally takes a considerable period of time for the draft of a proposed pronouncement to work its way up through varying levels of denominational committees until it is finally ready for action by the highest judicatory. There is, too, a vigorously maintained tradition of freedom of speech, especially by those denominations that claim to have invented the doctrine. Finally, the delegates or commissioners, while for the most part not experts on anything in particular, are drawn from the active membership of their church and do therefore have some clear notions of rank-and-file thinking. These considerations having been noted, it is still not possible to say with certainty—any more than it is with Congress—that what is voted represents the views of a clear majority of the constituents.

This leads to a related question: How responsive should governing bodies be to grass-roots pressures? Even granting that plebiscites are normally not desirable (conceivably a referendum to abolish all taxes might be approved by the electorate on a given day!) and are not usually practiced by the church fathers, should the highest church councils swing toward the political action programs favored by their constituents? To pose the question is to demonstrate the impossiblity of any precise answer. There is the added complication that almost any ecclesiastical official would resist publicly expressed pressures and declare, in effect: "We should do what is right, not what is popular!" Even so, there are numerous examples of the churches belatedly discovering the wishes of their parishioners and galloping to catch up with them. It cannot be entirely coincidental that the United Presbyterian Church has dropped its advocacy of Prohibition as the one and only approach toward drinking, nor that the Episcopal Church has decided that there is some merit in "social" drinking. More dramatic was the successful effort during the summer of 1963 by a group of Negro ministers to wrest the leadership of the Negro civil-rights drive in Brooklyn from the NAACP, CORE, the Urban League, and other secular organizations. The evidence, too, is increasing that the Roman Catholic Church is re-examining its attitudes on birth control, partly because of the insistence of some parishioners and partly because of the world population explosion.

THE PLACE OF POLITICAL ACTIVISM

Churches may hold very exact and very expert views on matters close to their hearts or purse strings, such as the management of municipal social agencies or tax exemption of church-owned property. Yet their expertise seems to wane as political and social issues become more complex and the solutions more elusive. It would be strange if the situation were otherwise, for in that case we could do away with the politicians who manage civil government and replace them with seasoned theocrats. To say this is not to disparage in the slightest the role played by the churches. Their contributions to politics are obviously of value, but they also contain certain inherent limitations. Some of these limitations are peculiar to the churches; others apply to all the great interest groups of modern, pluralistic society.

In American politics, the churches normally follow; they rarely lead. They usually react; they only infrequently seize the initiative. They have shown no sustained desire to dictate governmental policy, nor have they normally mobilized more than a small fraction of their total resources for political action. They have invested sizable amounts of money in education to affect the moral, social, and political climate of the country, but only a handful of dollars has been invested in specialists to influence the legislatures and the regulatory agencies.

The churches of America have elected to stress the judgmental role—which is really what a bishops' message or a social pronouncement amounts to—and to relegate direct political activism to a secondary or tertiary place in the repertoire. This attitude has proved so far to be helpful to politics, and it must be presumed that the churches believe it beneficial to themselves. And there is the further advantage that this outlook fits in well with democratic political theory.

CHAPTER SIX

Religious Influences on Elections

Religion is a force that has been omnipresent throughout American electoral history, and no political analysis would be complete without some assessment of its importance. Yet because its influence has varied from election to election and from region to region, it is difficult to deal with except in fairly general terms.

It is convenient and logical, as well as historically valid, to start with the political party that is based primarily on religion. That there have been such parties in the American past is hard to remember, for we are accustomed to believe that the major parties are all things to all men. The Know-Nothings of the 1840's and 1850's, for example, were not; they were Protestants who were violently anti-foreigner and anti-Catholic.

The Know-Nothing movement began in Louisiana about 1841, following an influx of aliens to New Orleans. The movement spread to the North, especially to New York City, where after an initial success it waned, later to be revived—first as a secret society, then as a political party. The progressive decay of the Whigs as a national party provided a vacuum that the Know-Nothing party was eager to fill. Scott's defeat in 1852—as Wilfred E. Binkley has pointed out—acted as a stimulus for both Southern and Northern Whigs to leave their party and "by hundreds of thousands" to join the American, or Know-Nothing, party.[1] The Know-Nothings reached their peak of popularity in 1854 when, for example, in Massachusetts they carried the governorship, every state senatorial seat, and a large majority of the lower house.

It was widely believed that the Know-Nothings would become the new party of opposition to the Democrats and that their chances of carrying the Presidency in 1856 were good. However, at the very height of their power, they split over the issue of slavery in their 1855 convention. Some fifty Northerners walked out after Southern politicians had rammed through various proslavery resolutions. The Know-Nothings became strictly a Southern party. In 1856 their Presidential nominee, ex-President Fillmore, received only eight of the necessary 149 electoral votes. As a party the Know-Nothings then disappeared.

Though the Know-Nothings are the only example in American political history of a large-scale party based in large part on religion, in this case a kind of nativist-racist Protestantism, the spirit of this Protestantism—anti-Catholic, anti-Jewish, anti-foreign—continued to be a factor in American political life.

Under the banners of the Ku Klux Klan, the nativist-racist Protestant movement flourished after the First World War. The Klan's exact membership is not known but it claimed four to five million members. Peter Odegard has made the point that the Klan held a balance of power in many states in the mid-1920's and was powerful enough to elect governors and legislators in "significant numbers."[2] In states such as Maine, Texas, Indiana (especially in Indianapolis), Alabama, and Arizona, the Klan was especially strong and active. The Klan was widely discredited, especially in the Midwest, by the indictment and conviction of many of its officers for crimes, and it rapidly lost its vitality. By the time America entered the Second World War the Klan was mostly a bitter memory, and postwar efforts to revive the Klan in the South failed.

The rising wave of Negro expectations following the 1954

school desegregation cases stimulated a revival of the always latent white Southern racism, this time in the form of White Citizens Councils, which spread rapidly throughout the South in an effort to prevent Negroes from enjoying rights to which the courts said they were entitled. In some states the political elite that controlled the dominant Democratic party had little truck with the Councils. In other states, especially in Mississippi, the Council movement permeated and dominated the state government on the issue of Negro rights.

The Know-Nothings, the Ku Klux Klan, and the White Citizens Councils represent the most extreme open identifications between religion and large-scale political parties or movements. It is more than coincidence that the electoral results of such unions have been uniformly illiberal and reactionary, since frequently—as Franklin H. Littell has maintained—the objective has been to return to a white Protestant America that probably never really existed outside men's willful imaginations.[3]

It is important, however, that these political movements based on religion be kept in proper historical perspective. They have not in fact succeeded in overthrowing the national two-party system nor have they in the last hundred years been able to take over a major national party. They have, to be sure, enjoyed local and state-wide electoral successes, but they have not been able to coalesce into a major electoral grouping. They have shown very little ability to organize on other than a day-to-day basis. Lacking organization, they have been transient and amorphous in comparison with the long-lived political parties, and have been more of a threat than a real force.

Americans who subscribe to the ideals of the democratic process of government—who are in the overwhelming majority—may be thankful that political extremists who base their movements on religious bigotry have usually been confined to fringe groups. It is only fitting, though, to note that it has been the American people themselves—whose attitudes in the long run make possible the effectiveness of institutions—who have insisted that their political parties be considerably more than the civic manifestations of religious affiliation.

THE RELIGIOUS AFFILIATION OF CANDIDATES

On the other hand, the electorate usually insists that candidates for public office be openly and clearly identified with a specific religious faith.[4] Church membership, too, must be more than nominal: there must be public evidence that the candidates take their membership seriously. Under these modern criteria Lincoln would never have been nominated in 1860 and in 1864.

Positive religious affiliation is necessary for a candidate, but more importantly this affiliation must be of the proper kind. Prior to the 1928 national Democratic nominating convention, when Governor Alfred E. Smith was nominated, it was generally believed in political circles that no Catholic could receive the Presidential nomination. Smith's subsequent failure to win the election and in particular his loss of several traditionally Democratic states in the Solid South led political pundits to reword their formula on Catholicism. It was then asserted that while a Catholic might be given the nomination in a year when it was certain he could not win, no Catholic nominee could capture the Presidency. If a national party were serious, it would not nominate a Catholic candidate for the nation's top office.

This proposition was said to be proved beyond reasonable doubt by the 1928 Presidential election, and for several succeeding nominating conventions it was unchallenged by either major party. The idea that a successful Presidential candidate had to be a Protestant, while by no means new in popular thinking, was elevated to the role of a concept as textbook writers included it under "the principle of availability," which listed characteristics that a candidate should or should not have. It was never meant to be ironclad, but its inclusion of the extra-legal disqualification of Catholics caused many a Catholic reader to wonder whether he was in fact a first-class citizen.

This "unwritten religious qualification for the Presidency" came under serious scholarly scrutiny insofar as the evidence to support it rested mainly on the 1928 Presidential election.

Long before the 1960 nominating conventions a number of leading scholars, including Peter Odegard, had concluded that Smith's Catholicism was by no means the "dominant" or "decisive" factor in his defeat.[5] There were more important factors, including the generally held belief that any Democrat would have lost in 1928!

As the 1960 nominating conventions approached, supporters of Senator John F. Kennedy made private studies to assess the probable influence of the Catholic factor on his candidacy. The results, especially those reported by John Bailey, a leading Democratic spokesman, showed that Kennedy's Catholicism might on balance be an asset instead of a liability, that losses in certain Protestant areas would be more than offset by gains in areas with large Catholic populations. As a result, Kennedy would benefit in the electoral college totals.

Once their candidate had received the Democratic nomination, the Kennedy forces proceeded to make an all-out effort to neutralize the religious issue. An important move was to appoint James W. Wine, who thereupon resigned as associate general secretary for interpretation of the National Council of Churches, to head a community relations committee in the Kennedy headquarters. Earlier in 1960 Wine had led a successful campaign to have the Air Force remove a manual that in part questioned the patriotism of the old-line Protestant churches. The objectionable materials had been introduced into the manual by a Protestant right-wing religious extremist, and the Air Force had accepted them without challenging their source or accuracy. It was Wine who exposed the right-wing origin of the materials. When Wine—the chief strategist in the National Council's spirited campaign to have the manual withdrawn—received a public apology from the Air Force, he immediately became known outside purely religious circles. It was natural for the Kennedy camp to enlist his expert support. During the campaign, Wine and his deputies crisscrossed the country, fighting Protestant bigotry through rallies, advertisements, and endorsements of Kennedy by prominent local clergy.

The most spectacular single effort made by Kennedy to neutralize his religion as a serious issue was his appearance at a give-and-take session before the ministers of Houston. Before batteries of television cameras the Democratic candidate delivered a prepared speech and then answered scores of questions which, though politely asked, were full of distrust and suspicion. The Kennedy strategists did not expect to make pro-Kennedy men of the ministers of Houston, but they did succeed in their primary objectives: they proved that Kennedy could calmly and effectively reply to the most complex church-state issues and that he subscribed to a strict construction of the religious clauses of the First Amendment.

Throughout the rest of the campaign Kennedy's remarks to the ministers of Houston bore tremendous dividends. Films of the dialogue were shown throughout the South, in an effort to demonstrate that the Massachusetts Senator's Catholicism could not possibly adversely affect him in the Presidential role. (The Senator was so convincing that many a Catholic observer growled that Kennedy was becoming more Protestant than the Protestants!) In addition, the Democrats showed them repeatedly to Northern Catholic audiences, where the standard reaction was one of utter indignation that Kennedy had felt it necessary to defend his Catholicism before the ministers. In this fashion the address and comments delivered at Houston gained support from Protestants in the South and from Catholics in the North—as neat a bit of politicking as the country had seen in many a day.

The religious issue in the 1960 election remained mostly submerged. It was one thing for the Kennedy forces to establish the position of their candidate on such questions as aid for parochial schools (he opposed it on constitutional grounds); it was a different matter for them to combat a flood of anonymous, vicious, often obscene, anti-Catholic publications. Fortunately, a nonpartisan organization devoted to fair play—the Fair Campaign Practices Committee—issued reports from time to time on the extent of such materials, and these reports received wide public attention. In addition, the Republican candidate, Richard M. Nixon, went to great lengths to disassociate his party from such attacks on Kennedy's religion. Nevertheless, the tide of anti-Catholic publications continued to rise until election day.

It is safe to presume that books written about the 1960 election will give due recognition to the religious factor. In the meantime, there is James A. Michener's *Report of the County Chairman*, the vivid assessment by a famous novelist turned amateur politician of the role played by religion at the grass-roots level of the campaign.[6] He found that the religious issue "permeated" every meeting he conducted in Bucks County, Pennsylvania, and he encountered it everywhere as he barnstormed in other parts of the country. As Michener reports the progress of the campaign, he gives his readers a series of vignettes showing the complex, and often confused, feelings voters had about Kennedy's Catholicism. The *Report* is probably the best running account of a Presidential campaign in the whole library of American politics.

John F. Kennedy received 303 electoral votes, Richard M. Nixon 219. The Kennedy total in popular votes exceeded that of the Republican candidate by only about 119,000 votes. Because several minor parties put forth their own tickets, the popular vote for Kennedy was only a plurality of all the votes cast. When a comparison is made of the returns for Kennedy with the returns for Democratic Congressional candidates, it is quite clear that Kennedy ran on the average well behind the level of the Democratic ticket. It is generally conceded that Catholicism was clearly the most apparent factor—in Kennedy's failure to keep up with other Democratic candidates.

The 1960 Presidential election was in no sense a referendum on Catholicism. Yet an implication of the Kennedy victory was that the electorate found Catholicism no more subversive of "Americanism" than it did the Quaker religion of Vice-President Nixon. Catholicism had finally joined the American culture!

Whether other religious groups will do the same remains to be seen. It depends, of course, on what one considers acceptable religious practice. Ordinarily, we expect that religious precepts, to be acceptable, should be consonant with the fundamentals of what Gunnar Myrdal called the American Creed;[7] among these fundamentals is a belief in the basic equality of all men regardless of race, and equal justice before the law. A religious group that subscribed to any form of racial superiority might reasonably expect that its adherents would be at an electoral disadvantage in those parts of the country where such a view on race was not shared. Even if a candidate in effect disavowed racist aspects of his faith, he could hardly expect to avoid the charge of racism as a campaign issue.

This situation would not ordinarily arise, for all major-party candidates for the Presidency and Vice-Presidency have been members of churches that—however they may behave in practice—have in our time repeatedly affirmed their opposition to racism. An interesting exception could be the candidacy of a member of the Church of Latter-day Saints, or Mormons, whose doctrine relegates Negroes to an inferior religious status, now and throughout eternity.

THE RELIGIOUS AFFILIATION OF VOTERS

For nearly twenty-five years sociological studies of American voters have indicated that there is a definite correlation between religious affiliation and party preference.[8] In a way, ward politicians have always known this; indeed, a good deal of the more colorful literature on American politics is concerned with the ethnic-based urban "machine," and with the assumption that goes with it of voting by ethnic blocs.

To many observers, a high correlation between religion and party affiliation was merely a natural result of immigration. It was easy to explain that for economic and psychological reasons Irish immigrants of the 1840's and 1850's rushed into the arms of the Democratic party, and it was simple to extend this type of logic to other immigrant groups. According to this approach, the relationship between religion and party preference was misleading and accidental, and the assumption was that it would become less pronounced as the American melting pot continued to produce an ever more homogeneous population. In the very long run, therefore, religion as an independent factor affecting political party preference would be expected to disappear.

Another explanation attributes the observed relationship between religious affiliation and party choice to the economic or class standing of the voters. Religion, it was argued by the proponents of the class thesis, should be considered to be less important than class standing in determining voters' affiliations. The argument by no means depends upon a crude trichotomy of Protestant, Catholic, and Jew, and the relating of each group to party preference. It is easily possible to take the Protestant category, break it down by denominations, and relate the denominational to economic levels, and the economic levels to party choice. For instance, it comes as no great shock to discover that Episcopalians in Northern cities tend to vote Republican and to be above average in income, or that Baptists in the same cities (very many of whom, of course, are Negro) tend to vote Democratic and to be below average in income; this seems to mean that income level is more significant than denominational affiliation.

The theoretical problem—as has now become evident—is whether religion is a force by itself in determining party preference or whether it simply reflects the pull of socioeconomic or ethnic forces or both. Is religion an independent variable or a dependent one in helping to determine the party preference of voters? The dominant opinion of the researchers—from Paul Lazarsfeld to Gerhard Lenski—is that religious affiliation is—in Lenski's words—"an important factor influencing the party affiliation of present-day Americans."[9] In short, while religion is associated with other factors in the question of party choice, it stands out consistently enough so that it can be identified in its own right.

Most sociologists are unwilling to go beyond a statement of this sort, for the evidence from the various voting behavior studies is never precisely comparable and there is always a chance of giving undue meaning to the findings of any one examination. Lenski, however, has speculated about future trends on the basis of the data from his 1958 metropolitan

Detroit survey. He reported that the data suggested that the political preferences of the religious groups he studied were becoming more pronounced with the passage of time. Along with other considerations, this one led Lenski to believe that there may be a drift toward compartmentalization along socioreligious lines in American life. The significance of this observation becomes clear if one considers contemporary Holland or Lebanon, where the major institutions of society—political parties, education, labor, and even business—are very often identified with religious groups.[10] Society therefore tends to be organized in terms of two parallel—that is, Protestant and Catholic—columns. Lenski suggests that if compartmentalization is the end-result *of* pluralism Americans might do well to study somewhat more critically than they have the arguments *for* pluralism.

A study of the 1960 Presidential election by Lucy S. Dawidowicz and Leon J. Goldstein under the auspices of the American Jewish Committee produced findings about the relationship of religious affiliation and voting that were consonant with those of earlier voting behavior analyses. Their study, *Politics in a Pluralist Democracy*, contains a section entitled "Jewish Voting Behavior" that furnishes new information on the voting characteristics of Jewish citizens. Of particular interest is the identification of Jewish voters with political liberalism. The authors state: "McCarthy may have pushed Jews toward the Democratic party as much as Stevenson pulled them in."[11]

RELIGIOUS ISSUES

Religious issues, or issues with religious overtones, may come before the electorate in a variety of ways. Most of these ways are indirect, since the electorate is not often asked by a legislature to pass judgment by voting in a constitutional or legislative referendum on questions of religious import. Also, the great majority of the problems are state or local, not national. In this respect, the proposals of the Kennedy Administration for federal aid to education—which Catholic spokesmen denounced as "discriminatory" because the proposed legislation excluded Catholic schools—were in a distinctive category. A much more typical controversy involving religious considerations would be whether the state legislature should authorize bingo or any other form of gambling, or whether a city zoning board should grant a variance for church construction.

In addition, it is important to realize that the gravest issues of church-state relations are usually handled at some distance from the electorate, and to recall that the basic church-state arrangement of the First Amendment was voted into effect by Congress and by state legislatures more than one hundred and seventy years ago. What the First Amendment means to subsequent generations is determined by the Supreme Court, whose members are appointed by the President with the advice and consent of the Senate. State constitutions also have the effect of removing from current politics the most basic of church-state issues. In short, the allegation that separation of church and state is being violated is usually referred to the courts for settlement along constitutional lines.

There are those who are willing to pounce upon all suspected of violating church-state barriers. Usually these guardians of constitutional purity are members of nonpartisan voluntary societies, although occassionally they may be individuals acting alone. Protestants and Other Americans United for the Separation of Church and State is always on the outlook for Catholic violations. Despite its title and the presence of various ministers on its governing boards, the POAU appears to be a completely secular organization built on the principles of humanism and dedicated to the proposition that government should be neutral in all matters of religion. Many observers, going even further, would consider POAU to be essentially antireligious in character, and therefore tend to discount its findings as biased. In support of their belief that POAU is strongly anti-Catholic, Catholic commentators have noted that several prominent ministers in the organization concluded after "studying" the question of Catholicism during the 1960 campaign that Kennedy was unacceptable for President because his Catholicism meant he could not if elected obey the Constitution!

In contrast to the controversial POAU stands the ideologically neutral National Conference of Christians and Jews, founded in 1928 by Charles Evans Hughes, Newton D. Baker, S. Parkes Cadman, Roger W. Straus, Carlton J. H. Hayes, and other well-known public figures. It is "a civic organization of religiously motivated people, seeking through education and discussion to promote civic cooperation and mutual understanding among men of good will of all religious and ethnic groups without compromise of religious beliefs."[12] Again, in contrast to POAU, which is dominated by Protestant ministers, NCCJ is headed by officers and staff who are laymen.

With a budget of approximately three million dollars and some 65 regional offices in addition to headquarters personnel in New York City, the NCCJ concentrates its efforts upon a wide variety of educational endeavors, including community relations, youth programs, and labor-management programs. Through Religious News Service, its international news agency, the organization furnished dispatches and photographs during 1963 to more than 450 publications and more than 200 radio and TV stations. According to the report of its president, Lewis Webster Jones, the NCCJ received some 61 per cent of its 1963 income from corporations, individuals, and foundations that supported fund-raising dinners, while an additional 22 per cent came from general contributions.

The American Civil Liberties Union seeks to protect religious liberty against infringement. This protection is nearly always sought in the form of court action to prevent a government or a private organization from engaging in an act the legality of which the Union is challenging. The Union is therefore frequently engaged in raising constitutional questions—federal and state—about existing state statutes and municipal ordinances. In terms of its construction of the religious guarantees of the Constitution, the ACLU takes what its critics call an "absolutist" position on the separation of church and state; that is, it upholds current Supreme Court interpretations of the First Amendment. The Union is not and does not purport to be in any sense a religious organization. It is therefore not offended if it is, correctly, characterized as being "secular." Insofar as religious liberty is a civil liberty, the ACLU has in recent years been one of its very strong defenders. Believers as well as nonbelievers have clearly benefited by the Union's efforts.

In the protection of religious liberties, state legislatures have usually been cast as villains, minorities as victims, and the courts—especially the United States Supreme Court—as heroes. Very often the subject of such litigation has been the conditions under which religious agitation could be carried on, as with the Jehovah's Witnesses cases. Another fertile ground for lawsuits has been the parochial school, and the most important questions have revolved about the extent of state aid.

In all of these instances, however, the electorate is far removed from the decision-making process, for it is the legislatures, and ultimately the courts, which are the battlefields. The electorate does of course act directly when it must vote in a referendum. (This happens in Massachusetts when the legislature prudently passes on to the voters the politically difficult decision as to whether to repeal or continue the laws against birth-control information.) With this and other arrangements there is no need to look for a conspiracy against the public, for it is characteristic of representative republics to assign the responsibility for settling issues to political parties, legislatures, and courts. And if it wanted to, over time, the public could overrule any of these institutions, a fact which is well known to the members of the institutions.

Religious issues tend to be deeply felt and emotionally charged. Despite constitutional fences and the understandable caution of politicians, questions with religious overtones frequently burst over the public consciousness with the unexpected fury of a line storm in Kansas. The divorce and remarriage of Governor Nelson A. Rockefeller of New York, in 1963, illustrates the complexities. The initial reaction to the announcement of the governor's divorce was one of restraint and sorrow; at the same time, there was considerable excitement and much public comment on his remarriage to a divorcee with four young children. Shortly after the marriage, news commentators for New York television stations interviewed "the man in the street" for his reactions, and so did several newspaper reporters. Amazingly, this public response was one of almost complete sympathy for the governor and his wife. Expressions of good will were the order of the day.

In contrast, and to the unmitigated delight of Rockefeller's political enemies, the ministry joined almost en masse in condemning the governor and by implication pillorying his wife. Even the president of the governor's own denomination, the American Baptist Convention, felt impelled to issue a public denouncement. The donnybrook lost its intensity only after the Rev. Dr. Eugene Carson Blake publicly warned his fellow clergymen that they were overplaying the divorce issue and making themselves ridiculous.

Shortly before election day in 1960, a series of events occurred in Puerto Rico that threatened for a while to undermine the position Senator Kennedy had been staking out on the separation of church and state. As late as mid-October, there had been no outstanding issue in the Puerto Rican election for governor, and incumbent Governor Luis Muñoz-Marín and his Popular Democratic party appeared certain to sweep the electorate. Then three Roman Catholic bishops issued a pastoral letter forbidding Catholics to vote for Muñoz or his party. By this act the bishops created overnight an issue of tremendous importance, for one of their points of protest was birth control, established as legal by the Statehood Republicans in 1937.

Governor Muñoz went to great lengths to point out that he had not initiated the government's birth-control program. Unmoved, the bishops counterattacked. In a second pastoral letter, Bishop James P. Davis of San Juan and Bishop James E. McManus of Ponce clarified their earlier warning and made it more pointed: to vote for Muñoz would be a sin. In the interests of absolute clarity, Monsignor Victor M. Nazario, McManus's chancellor, added that anyone who did vote for Muñoz "not only commits a mortal sin but can be excommunicated."[13]

The new Christian Action party, sponsored by Davis and

McManus, took full-page newspaper advertisements to remind voters that "Catholics cannot vote for the Popular Party." In view of such formidable clerical opposition in a commonwealth that was said to be more than 90 per cent Catholic, it was expected that Muñoz' usual victory margin of more than 60 per cent would be seriously reduced.

As it turned out when the ballots had been counted, Muñoz received 58 per cent of the vote and won a fourth straight term as governor. His party, the Popular Democrats, polled 456,000 votes, while the second highest party, the Statehood Republicans, received 250,000. The Christian Action party, which had carried the full and open endorsement of the Catholic hierarchy, managed to capture only 51,000 votes, less than the 10 per cent needed to stay on the ballot. From any point of view the Puerto Rican electorate had rebuffed the hierachy's excursion into party politics and had strongly affirmed overwhelming popular support for the traditional American concept of separation of church and state. Meanwhile, in the United States, other issues had overshadowed the remarkably forthright but politically immature actions of the Puerto Rican hierarchy, and there was no visible effect on the Presidential election. There had, however, been some understandably anxious moments for the Kennedy strategists.

RELIGION IN LOCAL POLITICS

Great constitutional problems of church and state before the Supreme Court and highly complex religiously related issues before state legislatures often have a syntax and a rhetoric entirely absent from local politics. In short, there is apt to be little glamour but a great deal of heat when a local clergyman denounces on lofty moral grounds some government-sponsored proposition or project which a rival clergyman has just praised. No matter how embarrassing the charges may have been, the normal tendency of most people is "to choose up sides," to support one faction against the other. What begins as a minor skirmish may turn into a major battle and divide a community for a very long time.

Any municipal government will ordinarily try hard to

avoid involvement in a conflict between religious groups, but it often happens that a conflict which was religiously inspired gradually assumes governmental dimensions. When one side or the other invokes the police power of government, the result is government involvement whether there is action or not. There has been very little real documentation of this kind of situation. A notable exception, however, to what might almost be termed a general conspiracy of silence is the examination of Protestant-Catholic relations in Holyoke, Massachusetts, by Kenneth W. Underwood in his book, *Protestant and Catholic.*[14] The study begins with an examination of an incident involving Margaret Sanger, who was prevented from giving an address on birth control in the First Congregational Church. Underwood then proceeds to examine in detail the relations of Protestants and Catholics to each other and to the total community, and everywhere the actual or potential role of government is evident.

In recent years the most heated and bitter controversies involving religious issues in local politics have unquestionably revolved about schools. These problems have been particularly acute in those areas of mixed religious population where the bulldozers and the birth rate have combined to render existing educational facilities inadequate. In their efforts to finance needed expansion of their educational plants, school districts have had to request tax increases and approval of bond issues. Quite understandably, there has been resistance from the electorate, especially where the cycle of rising expenditures seemed to have no foreseeable limit. Opposition to higher school taxes or to school-bond issues may come from many sources, but one source in the newer and religiously mixed communities has often been Catholic citizens who have felt victimized by what they call "double taxation," meaning that Catholic parents who send their children to parochial schools are in effect given two educational bills: one by their church and the other by the government.

Ordinarily the electorate is asked to authorize school-bond issues in a referendum, and usually it is asked to vote for or against a proposed budget submitted by the local school board. In most school districts the electorate also chooses the members of the boards of education, and here religious considerations may be paramount. (Even where the board of education is appointed, as in New York City, it is completely understood that religious "balance" must be achieved in the selection of membership.)[15]

There is a quality of undercover warfare in many—perhaps most—school-board elections in districts where the population is religiously heterogeneous. Where the religious composition of a district is constant, we can look for a stable kind of proportional representation—some agreed-on quota system—in the membership of school boards. But in changing areas—whether urban or suburban—a religious group that is on the increase (for example, Negro Protestants in Northern urban districts, and Catholics in suburban districts of Midwestern metropolitan areas) will usually insist on greater representation than the historic quota has permitted. It is at this point that the conflict is likely to come into the open.

There is nothing necessarily subversive of the public good in this procedure, but it is worth noting that it occurs in general outside the area of public discussion. Neither newspaper editors nor politicians ordinarily discuss religion in connection with elections to school boards!

THE POLITICS OF DECEIT: THE RADICAL RIGHT, COMMUNISM, AND RELIGION

The electorate—which is to say the politically influential segment of the general public—is constantly being bombarded with deliberate misinformation. But it is doubtful in terms of pure malevolence whether any campaign of recent years can match that directed against the old-line Protestant churches. Various right-wing extremists sought to discredit the political and social positions espoused by those churches and their councils by alleging that those Protestant bodies had been successfully infiltrated by Communist elements and asserting that the social pronouncements therefore followed a "Communist line." It is fairly difficult, of course, to take on most of the Protestant denominations in frontal attack at the same time. Therefore a convenient focus for the allegations of Communist infiltration was found to be the Federal Council of Churches during the 1930's and 1940's and after that its successor, the National Council of Churches.

Ralph Lord Roy, a scholar and Methodist minister felt it was important that these charges be examined in detail. In his book *Communism and the Churches* he sifted the amorphous "data" bandied about for two or three decades by professional detractors of the churches and found in them no tangible substance.[16] Roy's conclusions, in abbreviated form, are pertinent. He established that the Communist party in America "never did undertake a full-scale campaign to infiltrate the churches."[17] Secondly, very few ministers ever joined the Communist party during the preceding forty years —". . . possibly as few as fifty, perhaps as many as two hundred."[18] Those ministers who did join were mostly romantics or neurotics and few remained members for very long. Roy asserted that with churchmen as with other groups the main device used by Communists was the front organization. Only a handful of churchmen who joined front organizations were in any sense persistent fellow travelers, but those who were "severely injured the cause of social action in the churches."[19] Finally, speaking as of 1960 when his book was completed, Roy said: "Today Communist influence within the American churches is near the zero mark."[20]

What purposes were served by charging that large segments of the clergy and of church leadership were tainted with Communism? No doubt, the reasons are many and range from personal vendettas to pathological xenophobia. In the main, however, it is certain that an objective of most critics was to silence the churches, to keep them from speaking out on social questions. Failing that, the more limited objective was simply to discredit what was said. The idea of protecting political orthodoxy by restricting "freedom of the pulpit" is not new, and attaching a Communist label on clergymen in an effort to intimidate them goes back at least until 1930.

As a tactic, however, the practice of leveling pro-Communist charges at the principal Protestant churches and their ministers was taken over intact by the "radical right" groups of the 1960's. Just as the John Birch Society found "Communists" (never identified as to name or number) omnipresent in the Protestant clergy, so the Cardinal Mindszenty Society found "Communism" present among the Catholic priests of the nation. Whether the charges were true or not did not bother Robert Welch, the founder and *fuehrer* of the Birch Society, for he reasoned that if the Communists (the *real* ones!) were true to their own principles they ought to try to infiltrate the churches. Evidence that this had not happened was therefore dismissed as irrelevant.

The psychological and economic bases of the radical right—the feelings of dispossession, of rootlessness, of economic insecurity—have been extensively analyzed elsewhere,[21] and it will suffice here to draw attention to two related phenomena of the radical right: the close alliance it has as a movement with religious fundamentalism, and the sizable percentage of its leaders who are ordained ministers.

Fundamentalism in religion is a complex phenomenon and the term must be used with some care. It is largely an American development that stresses Biblical literalism, the authority of the Scriptures, personal pietism, and religious isolationism. It is suspicious of liturgy and ritual, of education (as opposed to indoctrination), and of all hierarchical religions. There is no apparent dictate in the inner logic of fundamentalism that would necessarily predispose its followers to political authoritarianism—there are many fundamentalists who are no more authoritarian in their politics than the average masses of the electorate. At the same time, there is a marked religious intolerance in fundamentalism that very often carries over into other aspects of life, including political life. Mostly, in short, the same people tend to be at once nativist, racist, and chauvinistic. They frequently use Protestant religious symbols at political gatherings; they invoke the deity on every occasion when they require outside help; and they find it easy to assume they are engaged in a holy crusade.

Many of the leaders of the right-wing religious-political alliance are clergymen and, in nearly all recent cases, they are Protestant. With few exceptions, they are members of fundamentalist groups or sects. The occasional clergyman who is also a member of one of the old-line denominations is a rarity, and it is safe to wager that he is regarded as a freak by his colleagues. It is assumed that he is either seeking personal vengeance of some kind or personal aggrandizement. No one knows for sure how much money is added yearly to the coffers of the minister-politicians who are so prominent in right-wing "crusades," but estimates run into many millions of dollars. It is also interesting to realize that the "foundations" operated by many of these same men enjoy tax-exemption privileges, although the organizations in question have often intervened actively in specific election campaigns. The only plausible explanation is that the Internal Revenue Service does not want to be accused of being against religion—an explanation that leaves unappeased many listeners whose political benefactions do not enjoy tax-exempt status.

It is difficult to estimate the strength of ministerial affiliation with the far right and even more difficult to assess its importance. The National Council of Churches calculates that the high point of influence in recent years was reached during 1961 and that it has declined sharply since. And indeed, it is worth recalling that in modern times the most spectacular examples of clerical leadership of rightist causes come not from the radical right of the 1960's but from the depression-colored 1930's. During the latter period Father Charles Coughlin, the Royal Oak, Michigan, priest, and the Rev. Gerald L. K. Smith were at their prime in espousing quasi-fascist movements.

An entirely new factor in the 1960's makes it unlikely that rightist clergymen will enjoy the popular followings they did in the 1930's. This factor is the emergence of Negro ministers into public life. As leaders in the increasingly effective Negro drive for civil rights and better employment opportunities, Negro ministers have suddenly become public figures deeply concerned with the realities of public policy. They are therefore in politics to stay and their collective influence is considerable. This influence works mightily in the direction of the fulfillment of the American Creed. It is probable that the clerical heroes in the political movements of the 1960's will be men like the Rev. Martin Luther King rather than the snarling self-proclaimed saviours of the far right.

CHAPTER SEVEN

Religion, Politics, and the Public Interest

Chief Justice Morrison R. Waite, in rendering the opinion of the Supreme Court in *Munn* v. *Illinois* (94 U.S. 113) in 1877, formulated the doctrine that business affected with a "public interest" was subject to government regulation. Justice Waite did not define the term but implied that it was associated with any inherently monopolistic enterprise—in the case in question, grain warehouses. As a constitutional doctrine, "public interest" has remained both alive and viable, and it has been used as a criterion in important regulatory statutes. However, since neither jurists nor legislators have defined the expression in any detail, it must be assumed that they have imagined the meaning to be largely self-evident. But does the term "public interest" bring to mind a sharp, clear image? Is there in fact general agreement as to the characteristics of this image? More basically, is it even possible for there to be a "public interest" in a pluralistic modern society such as that of the United States?

The answers to these questions are important, but they are not easily arrived at. There have been two extreme schools of thought. One has held, in the manner of Rousseau and Hegel, that the public interest (or "general will") is something over and above the particular interests that are visible in daily life.

Rousseau maintained that a basic distinction should be made between the general will and the will of all, and asserted that the former could never err. This is a kind of mysticism congenial to those who believe in the "organic state," but on the whole unacceptable to persons accustomed to the pragmatic Anglo-American approach to political philosophy.

In fairness to Rousseau, here is what he says:

> It follows from what has gone before that the general will is always right and tends to the public advantage; but it does not follow that the deliberations of the people are always correct. Our will is always for our own good, but we do not always see what that is; the people is never corrupted, but it is often deceived, and on such occasions only does it seem to will what is bad.
>
> There is often a great deal of difference between the will of all and the general will; the latter considers only the common interest, while the former takes private interest into account, and is no more than a sum of particular wills: but take away from these same wills the pluses and minuses that cancel one another, and the general will remains as the sum of the differences.[1]

At the other extreme is a denial that there is any such thing as the public interest. It is perhaps best illustrated by certain works on the legislative process, for example, Bertram Gross's *The Legislative Struggle*.[2] Gross and those who have adopted his approach view the legislative process as a naked power struggle where the strongest group or combination of groups wins. In this tradition, one would not say that the results were "good" or "bad," but that they were "inevitable," given the alignment of the forces. There is no room in this "realistic school" for such a concept as the public interest.

As a description of how legislation is actually passed, the realists are no doubt correct as far as they go. The problem is that they refuse to cross the boundary between description and prescription, between what has been done and what ought to be done. Even if the "ought" criteria are vague and hard to grapple with, they exist in men's minds. The fact that as a practical matter government must be operated on the basis of compromises of conflicting forces does not by any means do away with the belief that better yardsticks could be devised. When men say, "we agree on the objectives, we differ on the means," they are coming close to expressing a belief in a rationally determined public interest. It is not therefore necessary to inhale Hegelian opiates to believe that a public or general interest can exist which may differ from the sum of all individual interests.

This conviction that rational men can take a broad view of the factors in a situation and arrive at a rational and total assessment underlies the term "public interest." The fact that this is so does not mean that in any particular instance a governmental decision will necessarily be in accord with the public interest as so defined. It merely means that it is possible for this to be so, or to approach being so. Basically, it is only necessary to insist that standards do exist and that, in a general way, rational men can apply them.

THE CHURCHES AND SELF-INTEREST

It is an entirely different question as to whether or to what extent a particular interest group is able to express the public interest. Usually people are skeptical when a representative of the National Association of Manufacturers makes a plea for lower corporate taxes not on the ground that this would benefit big business but that it would benefit the general public. They are just as skeptical when spokesmen for the AFL-CIO advance propositions in the name of the general interest and only in passing for the interests of labor. All spokesmen therefore try to avoid making the kind of statement attributed to Charles Wilson (the quotation was only partial): "What is good for General Motors is good for the country!" (Wilson had also added, "and vice versa.")

The churches encounter precisely the same type of skepticism leveled at other groups when they support a position that will obviously aid themselves and maintain that considerations of the public interest, not of self-interest, have moved them to speak. At the February 1963 meeting of the General Board of the National Council of Churches, a statement originally drafted by a fund-raising branch of the organization was introduced, amended, and unanimously passed. The statement gravely warned the Kennedy Administration that proposed changes in handling tax-exempt contributions to voluntary agencies on the part of income-tax payers would jeopardize the future of the churches of America. In part the statement appeared to rest on the assumption that large contributors gave money to churches and other voluntary agencies in order to avoid paying taxes. The quarrel over tax deduction was later resolved when the Kennedy Administration for a variety of reasons withdrew its support for the offending proposed changes in the tax statutes. The churches have also found themselves in an ambivalent position in the field of broadcasting, an area regulated by the Federal Communications Commission under the theory that the air waves belong to the public.

There are two ways in which an organization may obtain time on the air. It may buy time directly, or it may receive free time from the station as a "public service." The buying of time is expensive, especially at hours when there is an audience of any size. Because of the expense but even more because of principle, the leading churches—Catholic, Protestant, Jewish, and Orthodox—normally ask for and receive public service or free time for those radio and TV broadcasts that they put on the air. Some smaller groups regularly buy time, and so do some individual broadcasters who operate on a free-lance basis. Though a few local churches own radio stations, the most significant share of religious broadcasting is carried as a public service, as has been especially evident in recent years on the TV networks.

Churchmen in charge of religious broadcasts, and radio and TV officials, have generally found it mutually advantageous to cooperate fully in the production and distribution of religious programing. Under these generally irenic conditions, it has come as a profound shock for the heads of the broadcasting businesses around the country to learn that church leaders are not always happy about the industry. In 1959 representatives of Catholic broadcasting and of the National Council of Churches suggested certain considerations that the Federal

Communications Commission might take into account when renewing station licenses. Industry spokesmen professed to find it difficult to understand how the churches, as recipients of the "largesse" of the broadcasting industry, could in clear conscience criticize practices followed by that industry.

Radio and TV executives, who had been soured by the churches' representations before the FCC in 1959, were once more upset when the National Council of Churches in June 1963 issued a pronouncement belaboring some of the important segments of the industry, including television networks and national advertising agencies.

The whole incident pointed up the ambivalence of the National Council's position in the area of broadcasting, and its importance lies in the fact that it was unavoidably typical of some other areas as well. On the one hand, the Council, through its policy-making General Board, not only claimed but also exercised absolute freedom to advise the FCC as to the practices and regulations which it thought would be in the best interests of the general public. On the other hand, the Council, through its subsidiary broadcasting unit, constantly sought from industry concessions as to air time and programing in order more effectively to serve the interests of the Council and its member denominations. It is perfectly possible to reconcile these different actions, but it is also possible to misunderstand them if one is not in sympathy with their over-all objectives.

The churches are in a very strong position to command public confidence when there is little ground for accusing them of self-interest. This situation is likely to exist when the subject under discussion is one of the really great issues of the day—issues that affect the destiny or happiness of all Americans—as opposed to issues in which the churches have a direct operational or business interest. To revert to an earlier illustration, what the National Council and some of the Protestant denominations said about proposed changes in tax deductions for contributions to voluntary societies sounded like self-interest. But when Dr. Eugene Carson Blake suggested on another occasion that it might be good for the country if the churches were to pay some taxes, he seemed to be talking on behalf of the public interest.

In other cases, too, the a priori assumption is that the churches are speaking to the general interest if the actions they are urging would result in government action beneficial to the great masses and blocs of society. In cases where a church body encourages action that appears mainly to protect its own private and vested interests the public normally and rightfully insists that the presumption of self-interest as the sole motivation of action be disproved. The public, or at least that part of it which is articulate, makes the same demand of labor unions, business groups, veterans organizations, and farmers associations. The churches are not singled out for special treatment, but they must be prepared to run the gantlet of public inspection when they talk about public issues.

THE CHURCHES AND THE PUBLIC INTEREST

The churches of America have expressed themselves on most of the great issues requiring political action that have captured public attention during the post–Second World War era. How each of the churches has chosen to express itself may be summarized as follows: The principal Protestant churches have for decades followed the practice of issuing social pronouncements, many of which call for government action. As a general rule, it is fair to say that churches in the Reformed tradition have historically shown a greater tendency to speak about such subjects than some other Protestant groups, especially the ethnically based Lutheran churches and the Episcopalians. With the formation earlier in this century of the Federal Council of Churches as the principal cooperative body of American Protestant denominations the center of attention tended to shift from the individual churches to the Federal Council. The establishment in 1950 of the National Council of Churches, as the successor to the Federal Council, heightened this tendency.

A pronouncement of the National Council generally carries more weight than that of a single denomination precisely because it is a collective statement of the representatives of 31 Protestant and Orthodox churches with a combined membership of more than forty million persons. In addition, under ordinary circumstances any pronouncement by the Council occurs only after a substantial number of denominations have already adopted a similar position. Therefore a Council pronouncement usually suggests a solid consensus.

Even so, the question as to the purposes and the permissible content of National Council pronouncements has continued to be troublesome. In an effort to clarify the situation, the Joint Commission on Ecumenical Relations of the General Convention of the Protestant Episcopal Church, in its report of January 30, 1964, made the following as Recommendation 3:

> We recommend these points to our representatives to the NCC: first, pronouncements, when made, should have as their primary purpose the opening up of issues about which Christian people ought to be concerned; second, pronouncements should be so phrased as not to bring into question the Christian commitment of those who do not agree; third, pronouncements should not try to give specific solutions to problems that must be decided by statesmen or others in specialized fields of competence. While pronouncements may be directed properly to any area of life, they should avoid the impression that they offer the only specific Christian solution to the problem.

In contrast to the Protestant tendency to issue what must seem to critics like a running commentary on current events, the Roman Catholic hierarchy in the United States has shown restraint and caution. A bishops' message issued on the occasion of the annual meeting of the National Catholic Welfare Conference deals with one subject. A typical example is the statement of November 26, 1959, which dealt with leading aspects of the population problem. There are no doubt many reasons why the hierarchy does not feel impelled to comment on the vast number of current issues that appear to require Protestant reactions. Whatever these reasons, one effect of the relative scarcity of messages by the hierarchy is to enhance the attention given them in the mass media.

Both Protestant and Catholic national organizations issue statements from time to time that are far less formal than social pronouncements or bishops' messages, for instance, in response to inquiries from the press. The key question in each case is whether the person quoted has authority to speak for his organization, or whether he is expressing only his personal views. Here, too, the advantage usually lies with the Catholics since they have less trouble than Protestants in expressing a corporate view. In some Protestant denominations, those both inside and outside the conciliar movement, it is virtually impossible to determine which individual has the authority between sessions of governing boards to speak on particular subjects in the name of the total group. As a result, a Protestant response in such a situation is likely to be formulated long after the issue has been forgotten.

Jewish religious organizations have been reluctant to address themselves in public statements to political questions. For such hesitation it is possible to find many reasons, but one of the most important is surely the fact that the number of Jews in the United States is not large relative to the Protestants or Catholics. Jewish political leverage is derived not from any over-all numbers but from urban concentrations of Jews in a handful of states that are pivotal and significant in Presidential elections, notably, of course, in New York. On this basis, President Truman's vigorous support of an independent Jewish state in Palestine is usually attributed to the Democratic need for New York State's electoral votes in 1948.

Secular organizations of the Jewish community have been vigorously engaged for many years in a wide variety of social causes, some of which involve political action. In the field of civil rights Jewish organizations have been second to none in their zeal and professional expertise. Jewish agencies have, of course, taken the lead in urging support for Israel. They have also tried to obtain guarantees that Jews would not be discriminated against because of religion in various countries, especially in the Soviet Union.

From these illustrations it is clear that the principal American religious groups have, according to their individual histories and traditions, spoken in a variety of ways about political problems. Logically, two important questions follow: Have the churches analyzed and urged action on the most highly significant problems? Has it made any difference?

It is one thing to observe that the churches issue a constant stream of pronouncements, resolutions, messages, statements, reports, and interviews on political subjects. It is quite another thing to inquire whether this never-ending flood of words has helped clarify the public interest on the basic issues facing American society.

A survey of National Council of Churches pronouncements from the inception of the Council in 1950 until the end of the 1960–63 triennium indicates that some of them dealt with topics of only passing interest. Looking backward, however, it is clear that many of the pronouncements (and resolutions) were focused on the major issues of the period. Pronouncements and other official actions on aspects of war and peace are numerous, and include recommendations on disarmament, nuclear testing, and the role of the United Nations. There are also frequent recommendations on problems of economic adjustments, including automation, unemployment, and pockets of persistent poverty. Social welfare, too, has been a major concern that is reflected in actions on housing, medical care, education, and the status of women.

All of the major church groups in the country have issued statements condemning the principle and the practice of racial discrimination. These statements appear in a variety of forms but their direction and their authoritative bases are absolutely clear. It is possible to cite statements of different assemblies or ecclesiastical leaders that were issued before 1941, but the great increase of public utterances on the need for better race relations came after the 1954 Supreme Court decisions invalidating school segregation statutes. In January 1963—it will be recalled—a tri-faith conference on religion and race was held at Chicago, and from this meeting flowed an impressive number of declarations by church and inter-church groups from national to precinct levels. Both the National Council of Churches and individual denominations had created by mid-year special "commissions" on religion and race in an effort to translate words into action. In particular, there was widespread tri-faith support for the Negro civil-rights march on Washington of August 28.

The churches, then, have tackled subjects of first-rate political importance even when, as with the Catholic bishops on the question of birth control, the issue was emotion-laden and the side taken was unpopular. Yet one curious additional circumstance deserves elaboration. Of all the great issues listed above where the churches took forceful stands regarding public policy, there was only one where the churches had it in their power potentially to set standards which the rest of society could follow. This was the issue of racial discrimination, where the churches in theory might have taken the lead over other institutions in society by vigorously desegregating their own establishments at all levels.

The anomaly facing church leaders was pointed up by a letter to the editor of *Presbyterian Life.* The writer, a layman, was reacting to news accounts that prominent Presbyterian clergy had deliberately sought arrest and had been arrested in order to demonstrate the injustice of certain Maryland trespass laws that kept Negroes from an amusement park. After condemning what the clergymen had done, the writer declared that his denomination, if it had to take "direct action," would "be much more convincing if it set up picket lines around some of our churches" where Negro Presbyterians were not permitted to worship with their white coreligionists.[3]

The actions of the clergymen and the indignant criticism of the layman both suggest a concern with the second question asked about church statements on political problems: Do they make any difference? As we have seen, even in the difficult and ambiguous area of race relations the answer is surely yes. Spurred on by a heavy sense of personal guilt, tired of being accused of hypocrisy and double-dealing, alarmed at the prospect that history would pass them by without notice, church leaders of all faiths diverted in mid-1963 a major part of their energies and resources to improving race relations. In doing so, they placed considerable emphasis on integration of their own local churches and institutions, and employed a variety of means, including substantial monetary pressures, in an effort to bring this about. Church leaders even went so far as to attack de facto neighborhood residential segregation, pointing out that it was at the root of a large share of school and of local church segregation. No doubt something would come of all these efforts—how much, only time and the attitudes of local congregations would determine.

The policy-making arms of the American churches have often run into internal and external opposition for what they have advocated regarding, for instance, disarmament or automation. But here they have not been hampered by corporate practices, especially in the local parishes, which went counter to the policies supported by the hierarchies. The churches are morally and juridically responsible for segregation in their local institutions, but they are not any more responsible for the solution of cold war problems than the Better Business Bureaus or the United Automobile Workers of America. Despite the obvious temptation such a condition affords for irresponsibility, the record of the churches is by and large devoid of abuse. More positively, it may be asserted unequivocally that the churches advocated steps aimed at lessening international tensions—for example, the treaty banning nuclear testing in the atmosphere, space, and underwater—which the United States government subsequently adopted. Furthermore, the churches played a significant role in educating public opinion as to why such steps ought to have been taken. In performing these roles effectively, the American churches were far from acting in isolation. The Roman Catholic Church took its leads from Pope John XXIII, and the principal Protestant churches were fully aware of the concerns for mitigating international tensions that had been voiced by the World Council of Churches and by the international confessional bodies.

There are many ways in which religious organizations contribute to the quest for the public interest, and one of the most effective is undoubtedly through sponsorship of journals of opinion. At their best, these journals are dedicated to the proposition enunciated by Mr. Justice Holmes in his dissenting opinion in *Abrams* v. *United States* (250 U.S. 616; 1919), where he observed "that the best test of truth is the power of thought to get itself accepted in the competition of the market." The "free trade in ideas" sought by the eminent jurist is the raison d'être of several relatively small but influential religiously oriented magazines of opinion. Such publications enjoy a degree of editorial freedom not normally accorded the widely circulated and heavily subsidized so-called house organs of the denominations.

America is a weekly magazine edited and published by a group of Jesuit fathers of the United States and Canada. Founded in 1909, the journal is published in New York and reported in 1963 an average circulation of 67,770. *Christianity and Crisis* is a very small (eight pages) bi-weekly published in New York by a group of editors associated with Union Theological Seminary. Established in 1940, it has a circulation of around 9,000 copies. Cochairmen of the editorial board during 1963 were Reinhold Niebuhr and John C. Bennett. *The Christian Century,* which terms itself "an ecumenical weekly," was established in 1884. It is published in Chicago by the Christian Century Foundation and enjoyed during 1963 an average circulation of 38,000. The influence of this magazine is far larger than its circulation figures might suggest, for it is an important channel of expression for cooperative Protestantism.

A voice for conservative Protestantism is found in *Christianity Today,* published bi-weekly in Washington, D.C. Paid circulation is put at 36,422, while what is called "controlled free distribution" is calculated at 139,138. The American Jewish Committee in New York publishes *Commentary,* an attractive monthly with a glossy cover. Begun in 1945, the publication has a circulation of 28,873. Also deserving a place of distinction among religious journals of opinion is *The Commonweal,* a Catholic weekly edited by laymen and published in New York. The magazine covers developments in literature and in the arts as well as those in public affairs, and is generally considered to represent a liberal Catholic viewpoint. It was founded in 1924 and has a circulation figure of 21,707.[4]

THE PROPER ROLE OF THE CHURCHES

The churches are in a position to speak to the public interest, and they have done so about the most important public (or in the broad sense, political) issues of our time. In the light of this, how may the churches most effectively relate themselves to the continuing task of defining and locating the public interest in areas of basic concern to the American people?

One method employed from time to time is for church leaders to present themselves before government agencies and to the organs of the mass media as spokesmen for their church constituencies. Often these constituencies are sizable, and the implication that they are in solid agreement behind their leaders is intended to create the impression of powerful mass pressures. Yet it is hard to sustain such an impression in the face of quizzical inspection by legislators, government officials, and reporters. The difficulty comes largely from the fact that there is no direct way of proving on a given political issue that a church leader reflects the thinking and convictions of his constituents. The churches do not hold referenda to establish rank-and-file opinions nor do they elect their leaders directly and according to ideological platforms. It is therefore very simple for a person who has not been consulted to say to a leader from his own church: "But you don't represent *me* on this issue." In short, the spokesman approach to the definition of the public interest is not especially satisfactory given the conditions of American church and political life.

Another method occasionally used by the churches in an effort to forward the public interest is for their clergy to take the leadership in building up popular support for a political position. As we have noted, the most successful example of this sort comes from Prohibition—"The Noble Experiment," as it was optimistically termed. More recently there has been the leadership offered by Negro ministers in the great drive for equal rights and employment opportunities. Both illustrations are unusual, for the churches by and large are not equipped for social action campaigns that are more activist than holding seminars or reading books. Furthermore, churchmen-politicians, who by definition are part-time amateurs, sooner or later must surrender whatever temporary reins of leadership they may be holding to the full-time professional politicians. At best, the churchmen can only assist the professionals in a push toward common political objectives. Such a contribution is important, but secondary.

There is another difficulty which applies to churchmen whether they appear in the role of spokesmen or as social action leaders. In practice, one group of religious leaders determines and enunciates policy on political affairs; another group is charged with the implementation of whatever course of action has been agreed upon. Such a division of labor is perfectly logical, but it has most frequently the effect of divorcing the policy-speakers from the policy-doers. Often long on ability but invariably short in number, these doers cannot possibly cover the parishes of the country except on a token basis. The separation is made all the greater when it is appreciated that churches ordinarily assign the responsibility for follow-up action in political and social matters not directly to local pastors but to specialists operating out of various church headquarters. It therefore often happens that a boldly proclaimed policy—one which may even make major headlines—may have little or no impact in the local parishes. No large American church has ever really mastered the techniques of translating what national spokesmen say into local action within a short enough period of time to make any marked political difference.[5]

If church spokesmen are somewhat suspect when they presume to speak on behalf of their constituents and if church leaders are relatively unskilled at the techniques of politics, how can churchmen effectively help to define and locate the public interest as opposed to the very numerous private interests of American society? It is submitted that the most satisfactory method for achieving this general objective is for church leaders to place their maximum emphasis upon the judgmental role of the churches. Such a role is excellently fulfilled by the American Catholic bishops when they issue and take collective responsibility for their annual messages. It is also illustrated by the social pronouncements of the leading Protestant denominations and of their cooperative councils.

When they exercise the judgmental function with responsibility and dignity, the churches have certain advantages which are not altogether shared with the other leading social institutions. There is the expectation that the churches are in a superior position to render opinions on the moral aspects of great political issues. There is an assumption of selflessness, of disinterest. There is the belief that it is proper for the churches to enunciate general principles while recognizing that the government has the responsibility for legislative detail and for administrative execution. There is the conviction that the churches have a broader perspective, a longer view of history, than other institutions. There is the very widely held presumption, in short, that the churches of America are in a unique position to speak to the public interest.

Notes

CHAPTER ONE

1. The Regents' Prayer case was *Engel* v. *Vitale,* 370 U.S. 421 (1962).
2. The Pennsylvania case was *Abington School District* v. *Schempp;* the Maryland case was *Murray* v. *Curlett.* The Court consolidated the cases in rendering its opinion. See *Abington School District* v. *Schempp,* 374 U.S. 203 (1963).
3. In a brilliant essay Philip B. Kurland has shown how extraordinarily complex are the constitutional problems of church-state relations, and how difficult it has been for the Supreme Court to state "appropriate principles to serve as means to agreed-upon ends." See his "Of Church and State and the Supreme Court," *University of Chicago Law Review,* 29, 1 (Autumn 1961), reprinted as No. 13 of Reprint and Pamphlet Series of the University Chicago Law School. A collection of very competent papers reflecting diverse viewpoints on church-state relations may be found in Dallin H. Oaks, ed., *The Wall Between Church and State* (Chicago: University of Chicago Press, 1963).
4. Associated Press dispatch from Montreal, printed in newspapers of July 15, 1963. The conference was attended by about three hundred leading theologians from fifty countries.
5. As cases in point, see the following: Gibson Winter, *The Suburban Captivity of the Churches* (Garden City, N.Y.: Doubleday, 1961); Peter Berger, *The Noise of Solemn Assemblies* (Garden City, N.Y.: Doubleday, 1961); and Martin Marty, *The New Shape of American Religion* (New York: Harper, 1959).

6. The *Yearbook of American Churches* is the primary source of statistical information on all faiths in the United States. Its founder and editor of the volumes for 1941 through 1964 was Benson Y. Landis. The compilation is published by the National Council of Churches, and Dr. Landis was an official in the Council's Bureau of Research and Survey from 1950 when the Council was formed until his retirement in 1963. The citations given in the text are from the *Yearbook* for 1963.
7. *Yearbook*, p. 248.
8. *Yearbook*, p. 280.
9. Robert M. MacIver, *The Web of Government* (New York: Macmillan, 1947), pp. 188–92. More generally, see J. Roland Pennock, *Liberal Democracy* (New York: Rinehart, 1950).
10. Dissatisfaction may stem from many causes, although theological differences are usually credited in official church histories. Secession of individual congregations from a denomination is the most extreme expression of dissatisfaction. In such cases both ministers and laymen are parties to the action.
11. See the essay by Alan F. Westin in Daniel Bell, ed., *The Radical Right* (Garden City, N.Y.: Doubleday, 1963), Ch. 11, "The John Birch Society," pp. 201–26.
12. To some extent an unsatisfactory double standard is involved when clergymen seek public office. The public seems to accept with relative calm the idea that it is proper for a Protestant clergyman to stand for some kinds of elective position. Yet the same public, or at least a highly vocal segment of it, could be counted on to shout itself hoarse yelling "violation of the doctrine of separation of church and state" if a priest or rabbi were to run for the same office.

CHAPTER TWO

1. See Roger Williams, *The Bloody Tenent of Persecution for Cause of Conscience Discussed: and Mr. Cotton's Letter Examined and Answered* (1644), reprinted in Alpheus T. Mason, ed., *Free Government in the Making* (New York: Oxford University Press, 1949), pp. 62–68.
2. "The Church Dare Not Be Silent," editorial in *Presbyterian Life*, 13, 10 (May 15, 1960), 16–19. The editorial concluded:

"We trust that Mr. Pew will tell these friends in unmistakable terms that The United Presbyterian Church and its General Assembly are not for sale."

3. *The Federalist* is a collection of essays written in support of the Constitution and distributed to different newspapers in New York State prior to that state's ratification convention. The writers of the eighty-five essays—Alexander Hamilton, John Jay, and James Madison—prepared their materials in great haste, and they presented a reasoned brief, not a balanced analysis. It is therefore remarkable that the collected letters are today recognized as among the world's political classics. The volume is available in many editions.
4. An excellent analysis of American value-systems may be found in Robin M. Williams, Jr., *American Society, A Sociological Analysis* (New York: Knopf, 1951). Williams develops with great skill the idea that dominant and subordinate values are in active competition.
5. For lively dissections of American "culture-religion," see the works of Peter Berger, Gibson Winter, and Martin Marty, cited in Chapter One.
6. C. Wright Mills, *The Power Elite* (New York: Oxford University Press, 1956). Many of Mills's books and articles irritated a large number of people. This book especially annoyed persons who, by Mills's definition, were members in good standing of the "power elite."
7. It may be *more* than an ecclesiastical principle that great denominations, no matter how large their income, always find themselves on the brink of financial overcommitment. The same phenomenon may be witnessed in many local churches which take literally the injunction to save the world. In both cases the impetus propelling these organizations toward possible insolvency is undoubtedly theological in nature.
8. Thoreau's essay "Civil Disobedience" was written in 1849. It is available in several places, but it may conveniently be found in Mason, *Free Government in the Making*, pp. 469–74.
9. The excerpts in the text from Randolph Bourne's *Unfinished Fragment on the State* are taken from the selection in Mason, pp. 701–09. For the complete text of this and other writings by Bourne, see *Untimely Papers* (New York: Viking Press, 1947).

10. John C. Bennett, *Christians and the State* (New York: Scribner, 1958).
11. Martin Luther King, *Stride Toward Freedom* (New York: Harper, 1958).
12. Franklin Hamlin Littell, *From State Church to Pluralism: A Protestant Interpretation of Religion in American History* (Garden City, N.Y.: Doubleday, 1962).
13. Willard L. Sperry, *Religion in America* (Boston: Beacon Press, 1963). The book was first published in 1946. Also Clifton E. Olmstead, *Religion in America Past and Present* (Englewood Cliffs, N.J.: Prentice-Hall, 1961).
14. Olmstead, pp. 59–60.
15. Sperry, p. 218.

CHAPTER THREE

1. See John Neville Figgis, *Studies of Political Thought from Gerson to Grotius, 1414–1625* (Cambridge: Cambridge University Press, 1907); Frederic W. Maitland, *The Constitutional History of England* (Cambridge: Cambridge University Press, 1908); Otto von Gierke, *The Development of Political Theory* (English translation by Bernard Freyd; New York: Norton, 1939). A good survey of political thought may be found in George H. Sabine, *A History of Political Theory*, 3rd ed. (New York: Holt, Rinehart and Winston, 1961).
2. G. D. H. Cole and the Webbs were prolific writers. For examples of their thinking, see G. D. H. Cole, *Guild Socialism* (London: Allen & Unwin, 1920), and by Sidney and Beatrice Webb, A *Constitution for the Socialist Commonwealth of Great Britain* (London: Longmans, Green, 1920).
3. Harold J. Laski, *Authority in the Modern State* (New Haven: Yale University Press, 1919).
4. Harold J. Laski, *Reflections on the Revolution of Our Time* (New York: Viking Press, 1943).
5. Figures from Littell, *From State Church to Pluralism*, p. 29.
6. *Yearbook of American Churches*, 1963, p. 278.
7. Will Herberg, *Protestant-Catholic-Jew* (Garden City, N.Y.: Doubleday, 1956). See especially Ch. 5, "The Religion of Americans and American Religion," pp. 85–112.
8. Bennett, *Christians and the State*; John Courtney Murray, *We Hold These Truths* (New York: Sheed and Ward, 1960).

9. Murray, *We Hold These Truths*, p. 7.
10. Murray, p. 8.
11. Murray, p. 13.
12. Murray, pp. 16, 17.
13. Murray, p. 18.
14. Murray, p. 23.
15. Murray, p. 23.
16. Murray, p. 23.
17. Murray, p. 23.
18. Murray, p. 24.
19. Murray, p. 24.
20. Murray, Ch. 5, "Creeds at War Intelligibly," pp. 125–39.
21. *Mater et Magistra, an Encyclical Letter of Pope John XXIII*, Donald R. Campion and Eugene K. Culhane, eds. (New York: America Press, 1961).
22. *Mater et Magistra*, p. 17.
23. A full collection of documents from the initial meetings of the Consultation on Church Union—the interchurch organization established to explore the Blake proposal—may be found in the Disciples of Christ occasional publication *Mid-Stream*, II, 4 (June 1963). The volume contains the proceedings of the Consultation at its two meetings in 1962 and 1963, held, respectively, in Washington, D.C., and in Oberlin, Ohio.
24. It must be emphasized that the movement toward Protestant unity through mergers of denominations has taken place *outside* the conciliar movement. There are two reasons for this: first, the constitution of the National Council of Churches prohibits that organization from having anything to do with such a movement; second, some of the denominations that have most wholeheartedly supported the conciliar movement at all levels are opposed to mergers involving their own churches. Even in the absence of a constitutional prohibition, these groups would be strong enough to block any merger proposals made through the National Council of Churches.
25. The statement was made by the Rev. James Gordon Gilkey, Jr., pastor of the First Presbyterian Church in Brooklyn Heights, New York, in an interview with George Dugan, religion editor of *The New York Times*. The story was carried in the July 27, 1963, issue of that newspaper, on page 20.

CHAPTER FOUR

1. The entire September 1958 issue of *The Annals of the* AAPSS is devoted to interest groups. For a résumé of and commentary on group theory as applied to politics, see the following articles in that issue: Oliver Garceau, "Interest Group Theory in Political Research," pp. 104–12; Alfred de Grazia, "Nature and Prospects of Political Interest Groups," pp. 113–22; Murray S. Stedman, Jr., "Pressure Groups and the American Tradition," pp. 123–29. The articles are in a section entitled "Toward a Group Theory of Politics."
2. National Council of Churches press release, January 2, 1962.
3. *Ibid.*
4. New York State Council of Churches, *Statement of Legislative Principles,* 1962 (Syracuse, New York), p. 4.
5. These and the figures that follow are taken from the 1960 *Annual Report of Church World Service* (New York: National Council of Churches).
6. The Sunday closing cases, all decided on May 29, 1961, were the following: *McGowan* v. *Maryland,* 366 U.S. 420 (1961); *Two Guys from Harrison-Allentown, Inc.* v. *McGinley,* 366 U.S. 582 (1961); *Braunfeld* v. *Brown,* 366 U.S. 599 (1961); and *Gallagher* v. *Crown Kosher Super Market, Inc.,* 366 U.S. 617 (1961). For an analysis of the cases, see Sister Candida Lund, "The Sunday Closing Cases," Ch. 8 in C. Herman Pritchett and Alan F. Westin, eds., *The Third Branch of Government* (New York: Harcourt, Brace & World, 1963), pp. 275–308.
7. On the Jehovah's Witnesses cases, see David R. Manwaring, *Render unto Caesar: The Flag-Salute Controversy* (Chicago: University of Chicago Press, 1962). In reviewing this book, John P. Roche declared that "Manwaring has strengthened my conviction that existing legal precedents have outlived their usefulness in the religion-politics area and that before we can cope with the intricate dilemmas we confront in education, public ceremonies and the rights of religious minorities, we must get some new categories." See *University of Chicago Law Review,* 30, 2 (Winter 1963), 406–15; citation is at p. 415.
8. The President's statement is available, of course, in many places. As might be expected, the National Council of

Churches follows very closely legislative and administrative developments in such areas of church-state relations as proposals for federal aid to education. A running summary of current highlights may be found in *Memo,* a bulletin published by the Council's Washington Office. For instance, President Kennedy's remarks on education from his second address on the State of the Union are recorded in *Memo,* 468 (January 15, 1962).

9. Quoted in *Memo,* 453 (April 1, 1961).
10. This pronouncement on public schools was adopted by the General Board of the National Council of Churches on February 22, 1961, at Syracuse, New York. The text is available from the Office of Central Records, National Council of Churches, 475 Riverside Drive, New York 27, New York.
11. *Ibid.*
12. Text in *Memo,* 453 (April 1, 1961).

CHAPTER FIVE

1. See Luke E. Ebersole, *Church Lobbying in the Nation's Capital* (New York: Macmillan, 1951).
2. The act to regulate lobbying is part of the La Follette–Monroney Act of 1946. It is formally designated as the Federal Regulation of Lobbying Act, Title III of Public Law 601, Seventy-ninth Congress, second session, 60 Stat. L. 839. For a thorough and critical analysis of the legislation see Belle Zeller, "The Federal Regulation of Lobbying Act," *American Political Science Review,* 42 (1948), 239–71. The constitutionality of the act was upheld by the Supreme Court in *United States* v. *Harriss,* 347 U.S. 612 (1954).
3. *American Jewish Year Book,* 64, 1963 (New York: American Jewish Committee, New York and Jewish Publication Society of America, Philadelphia, 1963), p. 435.
4. *American Jewish Year Book,* p. 445.
5. See the brochure, "National Catholic Welfare Conference," published by the NCWC in Washington and revised from time to time. The edition drawn on in the text was undated but covered activities through the year 1960.
6. "The Social Action Department," a pamphlet issued by the National Catholic Welfare Conference (no date).

7. *Ibid.*
8. Walter Lippmann, *Public Opinion* (New York: Macmillan, 1922).
9. Horton Davies, *A Mirror of the Ministry in Modern Novels* (New York: Oxford University Press, 1959).
10. *Ibid.*, p. 179.
11. Eve McFall, *The Case Against Eve* (Boston: Baker, 1963).
12. Willard Thorp, "The Religious Novel as Best Seller in America," in James W. Smith and A. Leland Jamison, eds., *Religion in American Life* (Princeton: Princeton University Press, 1961), Vol. II, pp. 195–242.
13. Thorp, p. 195.
14. Thorp, p. 195.
15. Thorp, p. 219.
16. See Peter H. Odegard, *Pressure Politics: The Story of the Anti-Saloon League* (New York: Columbia University Press, 1928).
17. R. Morton Darrow, "The Church and Techniques of Political Action," in *Religion in American Life*, Vol. II, pp. 161–93.
18. On the nomination of General Mark Clark as ambassador to the Vatican and his subsequent withdrawal of his name, see Dayton D. McKean, "The State, the Church, and the Lobby," in *Religion in American Life*, Vol. II, pp. 119–59, especially pp. 146–49.

CHAPTER SIX

1. Wilfred E. Binkley, *American Political Parties* (New York: Knopf, 1949), p. 194. A standard history of American parties.
2. Peter H. Odegard, ed., *Religion and Politics* (published for The Eagleton Institute of Politics at Rutgers, The State University, by Oceana Publications, 1960); introduction to Ch. 2, p. 25.
3. Littell, *From State Church to Pluralism*, especially pp. 147–56, but the critique of nativism is one of the themes of the entire volume.
4. The point that persons elected to public office are expected to have a formal religious affiliation is illustrated by the religious composition of Congress. A survey taken of members of the Eighty-eighth Congress, which convened on January 9, 1963, showed the following over-all breakdown:

	House	*Senate*	*Total*
Protestant	335	87	422
Catholic	88	11	99
Jewish	9	2	11
Not indicated	2	0	2
	434	100	534

There were 24 different "faiths" represented among the members of Congress. In the tabulations a family of denominations was considered to constitute a "faith," so that, for example, all Baptists were listed simply under the heading "Baptist." Methodists, with a total of 102 lawmakers, outnumbered members of any other faith. Roman Catholics were second, with 88 in the House and 11 in the Senate, for a total of 99. Members of Presbyterian denominations were third, with 82 communicants. The next few faiths in descending order were as follows: Baptist, 64; Episcopal, 64; Congregational, 24; Protestant (as self-listed), 20; Lutheran, 17; Disciples of Christ, 12; Jewish, 11; Unitarian, 10. The same survey also reported the religious composition of newly elected and of incumbent governors as follows: Methodist, 11; Roman Catholic, 9; Baptist, 8; Presbyterian, 7; Episcopalian, 7; Congregational, 2; Latter-day Saints, 2; Lutheran, 2; Disciples of Christ, 1; United Church of Christ, 1.

Survey figures were reported in an article by Roscoe Drummond in *The Christian Science Monitor* of January 9, 1963.

5. See Peter H. Odegard, "A Catholic for President?" in *Religion and Politics,* pp. 159–77, especially pp. 162–67.
6. James A. Michener, *Report of the County Chairman* (New York: Random House, 1961).
7. Gunnar Myrdal, *An American Dilemma* (New York: Harper, 1944). 2 vols.
8. A pioneering study that indicated a high correlation between religion and party preference was that of Paul F. Lazarsfeld, Bernard Berelson, and Hazel Gaudet, *The People's Choice* (New York: Columbia University Press, 1948). This was a study of partisan preferences on the part of Erie County, Ohio, electors during the Presidential campaign of 1940.
9. Gerhard Lenski, *The Religious Factor* (Garden City, N.Y.: Doubleday, Anchor Books, 1963), p. 142.
10. Lenski, p. 365.
11. Lucy S. Dawidowicz and Leon J. Goldstein, *Politics in a*

Pluralist Democracy: Studies of Voting in the 1960 Election (New York: Institute of Human Relations Press, 1963), p. 89.

12. This description of the NCCJ is taken from the 1963 "Report of the President," which was published as a folder and distributed to members of the board of trustees, contributors, and friends of the organization. The remarks in the next paragraph of the text on Religious News Service and on finances are drawn from the same report.
13. *Time* magazine, November 7, 1960.
14. Kenneth W. Underwood, *Protestant and Catholic* (Boston: Beacon Press, 1957).
15. Spokesmen for the three major faiths in New York City issued a remarkable statement on October 1, 1963, expressing dissatisfaction and "deep concern" because "religious communities are excluded from effective participation in the selection procedure," both for the city-wide and for local boards of education. The appeal was sent to Governor Rockefeller and to Mayor Wagner, and was signed by Rabbi Israel Mowshowitz, president of the New York Board of Rabbis, Msgr. John Voight, secretary of education of the Archdiocese of New York, and the Rev. Canon William S. Van Meter, executive secretary of the Department of Christian Social Relations of the Protestant Council of the City of New York. Under the law of New York State a panel whose membership is specified in terms of organizations submits to the mayor the names of persons who are deemed desirable and available for board membership. Religious organizations are not among those entitled under the law to have representatives on the panel. The religious leaders were demanding that their organizations be included along with the civic, labor, business, educational, professional, and community organizations which are specified in the law. See the account in *The New York Times* of October 2, 1963, and the charge that the religious leaders were seeking to violate "the spirit and the letter of separation of church and state" in a *Times* editorial of the same date.
16. Ralph Lord Roy, *Communism and the Churches* (New York: Harcourt, Brace & World, 1960).
17. Roy, p. 421.
18. Roy, p. 422.

19. Roy, p. 425.
20. Roy, p. 425.
21. See Daniel Bell, ed., *The Radical Right* (Garden City, N.Y.: Doubleday, 1963). Bell's essay, "The Dispossessed," pp. 1–38, explores the roots of the contemporary radical right. For a comparative analysis, see Seymour Martin Lipset in the same volume, "Three Decades of the Radical Right: Coughlinites, McCarthyites, and Birchers," pp. 313–77.

CHAPTER SEVEN

1. From Jean-Jacques Rousseau, Ch. 3, "Whether the General Will Is Fallible," Book II of *The Social Contract* (London: Dent, Everyman's Library No. 660, edition of 1913, printing of 1938), p. 25.
2. See Bertram Gross, *The Legislative Struggle* (New York: McGraw-Hill, 1953). This is a highly regarded examination of the forces at work in the lawmaking process. It is cited here as an outstanding example of the "realistic" approach to politics.
3. Letter to the editor from John S. Beck, published in *Presbyterian Life* (August 15, 1963), p. 4.
4. Circulation figures are from N. W. *Ayer & Son's Directory of Newspapers and Periodicals 1963*.
5. It is not altogether clear why the time lag is usually so great between the formulation of a policy position at the national Protestant denominational level and its workaday implementation through the actions of rank-and-file parishioners across the country. A reason often cited—poor communication through supposedly clogged ecclesiastical channels—will not stand up under inspection. *Any* denomination can very quickly reach its local pastors and through them the congregations, if it wishes to. This ability is demonstrated repeatedly when money-raising is involved. Another frequently mentioned and more plausible reason is lack of sympathy with the proposed action by some local ministers, with the result that a campaign gets under way tardily if at all in particular parishes. In theory, denominational leaders could by-pass unsympathetic local ministers by contacting laymen in charge of local action groups, but as a practical matter it seems unlikely that a denomination would undercut so cavalierly the authority of its ministers. There is a much more basic ex-

planation for the unwillingness of some local Protestant congregations to implement the policies proclaimed by the governing assemblies: these congregations do not believe in social action at all, or they do not approve of a particular policy. In practice, of course, what a congregation will be asked to do depends both on the pastor and also on the elected governing boards of the local church. It is obvious that in many cases local governing boards are much more conservative in political and social matters than are the highest assemblies of the denominations.

Selective Bibliography

American Academy of Political and Social Science. "Unofficial Government: Pressure Groups and Lobbies," *The Annals,* Vol. 319 (September 1958).

———. "Religion in American Society," *The Annals,* Vol. 332 (November 1960).

Bell, Daniel, ed. *The Radical Right* (Garden City, N.Y.: Doubleday, 1963).

Bennett, John C. *Christians and the State* (New York: Scribner, 1958).

Berger, Peter. *The Noise of Solemn Assemblies* (Garden City, N.Y.: Doubleday, 1961).

Binkley, Wilfred E. *American Political Parties* (New York: Knopf, 1949).

Davies, Horton. *A Mirror of the Ministry in Modern Novels* (New York: Oxford University Press, 1959).

Ebersole, Luke E. *Church Lobbying in the Nation's Capital* (New York: Macmillan, 1951).

Herberg, Will. *Protestant-Catholic-Jew* (Garden City, N.Y.: Doubleday, 1956).

King, Martin Luther, Jr. *Stride Toward Freedom* (New York: Harper, 1958).

Laski, Harold J. *Authority in the Modern State* (New Haven: Yale University Press, 1919).

———. *Reflections on the Revolution of Our Time* (New York: Viking Press, 1943).

Lazarsfeld, Paul F., Bernard Berelson, and Hazel Gaudet. *The People's Choice* (New York: Columbia University Press, 1948).

Lenski, Gerhard. *The Religious Factor* (Garden City, N.Y.: Doubleday, 1961).

Lippmann, Walter. *Public Opinion* (New York: Macmillan, 1922).

Littell, Franklin Hamlin. *From State Church to Pluralism: A Protestant Interpretation of Religion in American History* (Garden City, N.Y.: Doubleday, 1962).

MacIver, Robert M. *The Web of Government* (New York: Macmillan, 1947).

Marty, Martin. *The New Shape of American Religion* (New York: Harper, 1959).

Michener, James A. *Report of the County Chairman* (New York: Random House, 1961).

Mills, C. Wright. *The Power Elite* (New York: Oxford University Press, 1956).

Murray, John Courtney. *We Hold These Truths* (New York: Sheed and Ward, 1960).

Myrdal, Gunnar. *An American Dilemma* (New York: Harper, 1944). 2 vols.

Niebuhr, H. Richard. *The Social Sources of Denominationalism* (New York: Holt, 1929).

Oaks, Dallin H., ed. *The Wall Between Church and State* (Chicago: University of Chicago Press, 1963).

Odegard, Peter H. *Pressure Politics: The Story of the Anti-Saloon League* (New York: Columbia University Press, 1928).

Odegard, Peter H., ed. *Religion and Politics* (published for The Eagleton Institute of Politics at Rutgers, The State University, by Oceana Publications, 1960).

Olmstead, Clifton E. *Religion in America Past and Present* (Englewood Cliffs, N.J.: Prentice-Hall, 1961).

Review of Religious Research (the official journal of the Religious Research Association, Inc.; 3 issues per year).

Roche, John P. *The Quest for the Dream—The Development of Civil Rights and Human Relations in Modern America* (New York: Macmillan, 1963).

Roy, Ralph Lord. *Communism and the Churches* (New York: Harcourt, Brace & World, 1960).

Smith, James W., and A. Leland Jamison, eds. *Religion in American Life* (Princeton: Princeton University Press, 1961). 4 vols.

Sperry, Willard L. *Religion in America* (Cambridge: Cambridge University Press, 1946).

Truman, David B. *The Governmental Process* (New York: Knopf, 1951).

Underwood, Kenneth Wilson. *Protestant and Catholic* (Boston: Beacon Press, 1957).

Williams, Robin M., Jr. *American Society, A Sociological Analysis* (New York: Knopf, 1951).

Winter, Gibson. *The Suburban Captivity of the Churches* (Garden City, N.Y.: Doubleday, 1961).

Index